ENDORSEMENTS

Practical, pragmatic, ministry enhancing, thought-provoking and dynamic. Just what you would expect from a Modern Prophet who has gone through this process himself.

No prophet I know thinks they have made it. We are all still on a relentless journey of discovery in our relentless pursuit of God. Jesus is Big Country. The Kingdom is enormous. The beauty of God is still an awesome paradox. Both a close, heart-thumping reality and a far-off, all-encompassing dream.

There are many varieties of gift, ministry and effects. No one prophet does it all. However, true prophets are by definition explorers, pioneers, warriors, champions and game changers in their particular field of expression.

In the Old Testament, we see a prophetic concentration of the gift largely in a single people group. In the New Testament, there is a prophetic distribution across the planet. How we would prophesy in Africa is different to Asia and contrasting again throughout Europe.

It is vital, then, that people we are mentoring have access to a broad example-based learning that describes, defines and delineates the required identity, personality and spiritual growth required to be both tested and proven in this unique ministry.

To this end, Shawn's book *Modern Prophets* will empower every student of the prophetic to determine their field of expression, level of authority, and the requirements of gift, ministry and office as a prophetic voice.

I heartily recommend both the book and the man.

GRAHAM COOKE
brilliantperspectives.com

I'm so grateful to Shawn for writing *Modern Prophets.*

This is a brilliant and comprehensive combination of Bible-based teaching and practical wisdom in every aspect of the prophetic, while exuding God's overwhelming love toward people through Shawn's wealth of experience in this area.

I will be giving it to all our pastors as a vital reference for health and growth in our movement.

It's relationally written by one of the most credible prophets of our time, and everyone will benefit from this book and all the manuals and courses that stem from it.

MARK VARUGHESE,
Senior leader of Kingdomcity
kingdomcity.com

Modern Prophets by Shawn Bolz is truly one of the most thorough and solid handbooks on the prophetic and the role of prophets that I have read. It is inspirational, impartational, practical, and theological. This book should be in every believer's library. It is in mine!

DR. PATRICIA KING
Founder of Patricia King Ministries
www.patriciaking.com

Modern Prophets is a breakthrough work on the subject of prophecy and prophetic ministry. Shawn Bolz demystifies classic modern areas of confusion with exhaustive scriptural analysis and clear, concise teaching that will appeal to beginners and the experienced alike. He not only shows that the prophetic gifts were designed to be integral to our lives—he gives us practical, accessible models and tools for using these gifts effectively.

Shawn is a humble leader who is passionate about sharing what God has shown him to others. After decades in ministry, he continues to express his childlike delight in seeing God work through him to demonstrate that love is the divine heartbeat and purpose for the prophetic.

BOB HASSON

Business owner. leadership consultant, coauthor of *The Business of Honor* with Danny Silk

BobHasson.com

Church history is filled with stories of abusive and/or self-appointed prophets. Many avoid the subject out of personal pain or fear. Yet my story is quite the opposite. Healthy, loving prophets have been a huge part of my life for the last 45 years. They love God with all their hearts and demonstrate that by their love and compassion for people. Among them all, Shawn Bolz stands out in a very significant way, as he is a refreshing example of what God intends for us all in this next season. I consider him a dear friend who is also one of the most powerful prophetic voices of our time. His profound impact comes in part from his wholehearted acceptance of his task to "equip the saints." We benefit greatly because of how he has laid down his life to be a bridge to the prophetic for the body of Christ. With authentic love and humility, *Modern Prophets* seeks to do just that—to encourage, teach, and empower the church to manifest the love of God on Earth through prophecy. This book is filled with practical steps to fortify a healthy and mature prophetic community, both within and beyond the four walls of the church. We need this, as the unbeliever has an inbuilt hunger to be seen and delighted in by the Lord.

BILL JOHNSON

Bethel Church, Redding, CA

Author of *God Is Good* and *The Way of Life*

www.bethel.com

I am so excited to see what Shawn is developing for the prophetic ministry. The idea of the prophets and prophetesses being entrenched in culture and society in such a way to hear what God wants to do regarding complex issues and scenarios is something we all should get very excited about. I feel this is a blueprint of sorts for the prophetic ministry in the coming days. Be prepared to have your paradigm shifted as you read this book. I know mine has and I pray you see what it could look like.

ERIC JOHNSON
Senior pastor and author
Bethel Church, Redding, CA
www.bethel.com

The Word clearly shows that the highest and best prophetic gift is the gift of prophecy. The good news is that it also says that everyone can do it! I love how Shawn's book breaks down every tall barrier we may have built to keep this gifting unattainable. He is making the prophetic accessible again and empowering an entire generation to step into it in a fresh way!

SEAN FEUCHT
seanfeucht.com

Shawn Bolz in my opinion is one of the top-three prophets of our time. I've always said I'm most impressed with prophets who raise up prophets and the prophetic in communities. Well, Shawn does that perfectly. This book, *Modern Prophets* will honor the gift, the receiving community, and the office of a prophet. We need that today.

ROBBY DAWKINS
RobbyDawkins.com

Modern Prophets is a must-read for any believer who desires to go deeper with God! I have never read a book that so thoroughly explains prophesy, what it is, and how God speaks to us. Like most Christians, I knew God spoke in many ways, but *Modern Prophets* is like an encyclopedia of ways God speaks to us. It gives biblical examples of these ways so that we can be equipped to listen more intentionally and hear how God is speaking. God has given the gift of prophecy to all believers, and this book teaches us how to use it. *Modern Prophets* sets a powerful framework for how to build and grow the gift of prophecy in a healthy, loving, empowering way. It doesn't matter where you are in your walk with the Father, He wants to take you into a deeper relationship, and *Modern Prophets* is a key to open that door!

JON B. FULLER
Author, speaker, podcaster
Are You Real podcast
www.areyoureal.org

The gift of prophecy and the role of the prophet have been some of the most misunderstood and abused topics in the body of Christ. Consequently, the church has a tendency to avoid an incredible gift God has given us. We must not ignore the fact that throughout Scripture, the prophet and the gift of prophecy were instrumental in the plan of God for His people. The prophetic gift was introduced into my life during my late teens and has been a key part of my journey with God ever since. In his book *Modern Prophets*, Shawn Bolz calls the church to understand and embrace the prophetic, which God intends to use for our benefit and for those around us. As always, Shawn writes with authenticity and deep biblical roots. He does not shy away from the uncomfortable aspects of the prophetic while revealing just how beautiful and needed this gift and role is.

BANNING LIEBSCHER
Jesus Culture founder and pastor
jesusculture.com

When it comes to anything to do with the prophetic, I want to listen to Shawn Bolz. He has unique qualifications that seem to separate him from almost anyone else, making him essentially a hybrid voice. He is still young enough in both age and perspective to be looked at in terms of what is "next generation." However his decades of experience because of his early start with prophets and the prophetic make him also a seasoned father in the prophetic movement. He grew up with the renowned Kansas City prophets, learning and being mentored by the marquis names in the prophetic, and yet he did not stop with what the last generation taught and modeled. This book takes us from the ceiling of the last prophetic generation and gives us an important new floor to start from. I believe this book to be of immense value to the body of Christ both in explaining and defending all that is prophetic and, maybe more importantly, correcting the excesses and providing helpful administrative guidelines to facilitate the advancement of this powerful gift of God. Whether you are trying to personally grow in the prophetic or whether you are a leader trying to incorporate the prophetic into your church or movement, I cannot imagine a more valuable book. Read it all, as it gets progressively better and more important.

JOHNNY ENLOW

www.restore7.org

Modern Prophets is an excellent guide for readers seeking clarification and understanding of the prophetic, especially in highlighting its relevance today. Over the many years I've known Shawn and his family, I admire his genuineness and insatiable desire to know God more intimately. Shawn Bolz is a forerunner in prophetic training of all levels; this book exemplifies his passion to share with you what he is learning in fine-tuning his connection with God. From the office of the prophet to the daily equipping of the prophetic gift, Shawn shines light on the creativity God communicates through the prophetic and how to keep integrous standards of accountability, featuring relational aspects of prophetic encounters. Throughout history and in today's information-riddled world, prophetic revelations tap into the essence of God. I truly believe that *Modern Prophets* will equip you to commune further with the heart of God and deeper into your prophetic gifting and understanding. Allow God to grow in you, and experience your prophetic gift develop in every dimension of your connection.

Shawn Bolz is the epitome of a modern prophet! From back alleys in India to huge palaces in Africa, Shawn is delivering timely, accurate words from the Lord all over the globe, and helping to change lives, governments, nations, and institutions, one person at a time. Shawn has an incredible way of taking lofty theological truths and instilling them into relevant, relatable, steps that we can all apply in our walk with God and service to humanity. Shawn Bolz is a dynamic reminder that prophets still exist among us today!

MODERN PROPHETS

A TOOLKIT FOR EVERYONE ON HEARING GOD'S VOICE

SHAWN BOLZ

Published by ICreate Productions,
PO Box 50219, Studio City, CA 91614
www.bolzministries.com

To contact the author about speaking at your conference or church,
please go to www.bolzministries.com

Edited by Kyle Duncan

ISBN: 978-1-947165-75-5

eBook ISBN: 978-1-949709-03-2

Printed in the United States of America

DEDICATION

I remember when I was 17 I received a word from a pro-phetic man, Phil Elston, that I was going to be an Elisha to a movement and carry the current prophetic movement's bags around. Then this kind prophet said that the bags wouldn't be administrative assistance but their baggage both good and bad in their personal life and I would learn from them not only the glory of what the prophetic could be but also the hard parts of peoples' woundedness and humanity. This could never be so true looking at 25-plus years later in my journey.

I want to dedicate this book to the prophets who have taught me so much and with whom I got to actually do life in intentional relationship. I was blessed to carry the bags in this context of many people, sometimes carrying their hearts through offense, other times learning how to lead or hold my heart through their beautiful examples. These men and women, who seemed so empowered by God that their humanity sometimes couldn't be seen by the masses, gave me a front-row view by default of how they included me in their lives.

Thank you to those who God gave me to walk with so that I could learn by both your strengths and your weaknesses, which I think anyone who is really going to grow into maturity has to look at in an honoring way in both areas.

SHAWN BOLZ

www.BolzMinistries.com
Host of Exploring the Prophetic podcast
Author of *Translating God, God Secrets,
Keys to Heaven's Economy*

TABLE OF CONTENTS

FOREWORD
BY JOHN BEVERE

How do you know when God is speaking through another? Today, there is an insatiable hunger for the prophetic word of the Lord. Christians are eager to receive words from the Lord and to share them. However, along with the genuine desire for the real comes a vulnerability to excessive or counterfeit prophetic ministry. Therefore, it is imperative to understand both the purpose and function of the prophetic gifts and ministry and how to correctly operate in them.

Through many years of experience and much trial and error, my friend Shawn Bolz has learned to not only clearly hear from God but to also clearly speak on His behalf. In *Modern Prophet*, Shawn reveals how hearing from God is available today and how you too can be a vessel through which God speaks to others. By demystifying the fog surrounding the prophetic gifts and ministry, Shawn lays a solid scriptural foundation, thoroughly examining the multifaceted aspects of the prophetic through both the Old and New Testaments, while including many examples and lessons from his personal journey. Shawn also explores how the prophetic ministry is not exclusive to the church but extends beyond its four walls—infiltrating all spheres of influence, such as politics and business.

Unfortunately, there has been much confusion throughout church history surrounding the belief that God still speaks. Due to this, many have turned to the counterfeit, with the psychic industry profiting tremendously from people's innate desire to hear from God. Fortunately, we are experiencing an uprising of prophetic voices who have passed through the wilderness and are boldly declaring what God has to say! Shawn is one of those voices and has become a trusted and respected prophet throughout the body of Christ. You'll quickly realize that *Modern Prophets* is more than a book—it is a manual that will equip you with the tools you need to function effectively in the prophetic, regardless whether you're called to a prophetic office or not.

There is one universal and fundamental truth that is interwoven throughout this message: God loves to communicate with His children.

JOHN BEVERE
Best-selling author and minister
Cofounder of Messenger International

1 | GOD WANTS TO SPEAK TO YOU

This book starts with one central premise: *God loves to communicate with His children.*

By hearing His heart, intentions, and desires, we can see our world become a very different place. As I talk to other believers and travel to different churches, I often hear people say they don't feel connected to hearing God's voice. As a result, they don't understand what an amazing toolset the prophetic can be.

In other words, things about prophecy and prophets can seem inaccessible to the average Christian. And in some ways, today the prophetic gifts are placed in a niche category in the Church—seemingly reserved for a select group of folks.

I have good news: the realm of prophecy—hearing the voice of God in its many biblical forms—is available to every believer. While not everyone is called into the office of the prophet, that does not mean you are not a prophetic

1

person who can hear from God. We will delve into these differences within these pages.

My goal is that this book will help demystify the subject of prophecy, prophetic ministry, and the role of a prophet. My prayer is that whether you are in business and need a prophetic advisor or have been placed in a church as a prophetic voice, you will feel empowered to see these gifts change the world around you.

Even if you have just become a Christian, God may already be stirring up the prophetic gifts within you. If so, read on.

I love that as a Christian you are guaranteed to hear from God, and that many of you reading this already do! There is a big difference, however, in *knowing* we can do something and knowing *how to use the thing* God has given to us.

It's like listening to your car radio: just because you own a car that comes with a radio, it doesn't necessarily mean you know how to turn it on, tune into various stations, or control the volume level. The same is true with the prophetic: knowing you hear from God is different from understanding the biblical purpose of the gift, and being proactive in exercising it.

It takes time, focus, biblical study, and practice under the direction of mentors to accurately hear and effectively apply what God is saying about our lives, families, churches, and the broader marketplace.

MY JOURNEY INTO THE PROPHETIC

When I started growing in my desire to hear God, my whole life changed. Even today, after twenty-plus years of prophetic ministry, I still think I am opening new places of my prophetic curiosity. And I have so much more to learn—which is healthy! The more revelation you receive from God, the more you want it.

While I do have some expertise, I certainly don't believe I have learned the majority of what God still wants to teach me. Far from it; there is so much more I want to experience and know.

I am grateful that I was exposed to many amazing people over the years: some simply had a prophetic bent, others used prophecy in ministry, and some operated fully in the gift of prophet. It's like God exposed me to a full gamut of what was available. Many of my prophetic friends and the prophets in my life seemed to have an inherent "knowing" of the operation of their gifts. They seemed to know who they were supposed to talk to, what their sphere of authority was, and why they were prophesying.

In contrast, I knew very little. My pursuit of the prophetic gifts was not well thought out; I just had a hunger for them and ran after any materials that could teach me. I read pretty much everything I could find on the prophetic gifts, the office of a prophet, and the everyday use of prophecy in a believer's life. I was—and still am—so hungry to grow!

I love so much of what I found, but there always seemed to be a gap. For me, something was missing—like a whole conversation that bridged the teaching of the gifts and how to actually incorporate them into real life. I couldn't find teaching that showed me how to administer my growth in the gifts into my sphere of influence.

I had so many questions. What was my responsibility in the prophetic? What were the incentives and motivations I should be following? How could I find an authority structure and accountability process I needed in order to grow in my prophetic gifts?

No one seemed to teach these parts directly with real-world examples. I seemed to find all the teaching in the world on *how* to prophesy, but not about *who* to prophecy to or how to develop personal authority and spiritual relatability.

Also, I couldn't find teachings on how to develop other prophetic people. Friends and pastors kept telling me I was a prophet, but what was I a prophet of? Even when the movement I was a part of ordained me as a prophet, no one knew how to define my responsibilities. These uncertainties created confusion for both parties.

In some ways, I feel like God has given me favor in the prophetic ministry during this season to help reconstruct—or bring back—some practical tools of healthy theology and practice. In fact, that is my main reason for writing this book.

Recently, one of the leaders of one of the movements that I am a prophetic voice in had a conversation with me. For the sake of this conversation, we will call him Joe. He said, "Some of the best prophets in the world are in our movement, and I am just desperate to hear what God is saying for us. I want a Bob Jones!"

For those who might not be familiar with Bob Jones, I am referring to a different Christian leader from the person who founded Bob Jones University. Bob Jones was, however, one of the most well-respected, accurate prophetic voices of the twentieth and twenty-first centuries and who spoke into the lives of leaders and Christian movements for more than four decades.

I was blessed to call Bob Jones a dear friend. He was a man who carried the movements he was involved with in his heart and would regularly give them key revelation. He always went out of his way to be present with his gift in the lives of the leaders he touched. (It seems fitting that he passed away on Valentine's Day 2014—a day known for love.)

It was this amazing sense of love and presence that endeared Bob to many leaders and prophetic movements and that gave him strategic authority to help certain church streams and denominations go to another level of effective ministry.

Joe even felt a little guilty admitting that he yearned for a Bob Jones-type relationship for himself, because he was a leader and mentor over many other prophetic ministries. He was simply and sincerely revealing a disconnection between his leadership and the prophets under his authority. And though Joe was finding faults in some of the prophetic peoples' gifts, ultimately it was he who didn't have a model for administering those relationships. He was just letting things happen, using reactive energy and often operating out of the moment.

Indeed, some amazing things were happening in the ministries under his authority—but he wanted more. He wanted trained, seasoned prophetic voices he could run his plans and vision by and who could speak into his ministry to help save him years of trial and error.

He wanted to walk alongside these prophetic people and have them help position other staff members. He wanted to train his people to see visions and then have them help various departments develop blueprints to fulfill those visions. He had a heart for emerging leaders, whereby his prophetic team would provide words to help these new leaders set up their whole ministry life within the movement.

These were the types of examples Joe had seen and heard of, but he was yet to see things click prophetically for his administration.

I asked him, "When a prophetic person is brought into your movement, what responsibility does that recognition bring?" After he answered, I realized he was giving people a title or role but not really a tangible plan for implementing their responsibilities as a prophet.

The reality, however, is that if you want a person to be successful, then you must define the identity, responsibility, administration and role of what you are inviting them to do, or they have to help define it to you. So much of the prophetic has been undefined, or defined by needs that are not sustainable. Or even worse, the wrong types of people are placed into the wrong roles.

THE NEED FOR MODERN PROPHETS

Another friend (let's call him Peter) owns a very successful business and told me about an incredible prophetic word he had received that had moved his entire business forward. But now, after reaching a new plateau, he needed to hear God even more for the new, more complex challenges he was facing. In essence, the miraculous word that had helped catapult his business forward needed some fresh words of wisdom to flesh out the next phase.

Peter asked me, "Is it possible to hire or appoint a prophetic intercessor or prophet in my company so that I have someone to help navigate with me? Or is that manipulation?"

This incredible, mature Christian businessman, who is a kingdom thinker and very sacrificial, was worried about inviting in a tool set from God because he didn't understand it. Did he have a legitimate, definite need for it? Absolutely!

My experiences with Joe and Peter showed me that the prophetic movement is still on a learning journey on how to incorporate the prophetic into our world. We need to take the theory and make it practical—in church life, politics, business, the creative fields, education, the family—everywhere.

But if we were able to look at this tool set of the prophetic gifts and gain proactive energy and insight on how to implement and administer these gifts, both as individuals and as corporate groups, then what do you think would happen in the world around us? Radical transformation.

In my book *Translating God*, I help bring people to a love-based approach toward hearing God's voice. In the book you hold in your hands, I want to help build the theology of how to hear God's voice and what the prophetic gifts can do to benefit individuals and corporate groups. As well, we will explore how to administer these gifts and ministries—and even the office of the prophet—in your church or organization. I also want to give you some starter models for this purpose.

I am taking a semi-exhaustive approach as I look at the following key subjects:

1. the ways God speaks in both the Old and New Testaments;

2. an overview of prophetic personalities;

3. the fruit and incentives of the prophetic;

4. avoiding the pitfalls of bad practices and old patterns;

5. providing encouragement to help you include the prophetic in your very real life today;

6. help you find courage, confidence, and boldness in how you hear God;

7. and how to invite others to hear God and lead others in their prophetic journey.

This book and the e-courses that accompany it are about how to incorporate the prophetic into every facet of your life and ministry. My goal is to help demystify this sometimes niche discipline and gift so that it becomes a very real, useful tool in your very real world. I want you to feel so empowered in your understanding and use of the prophetic that you can't *not* include this wonderful aspect of God's kingdom in your life.

May the lessons we explore here together help you grow in a vibrant, trackable, personal prophetic history with God.

PART I

THE THEOLOGY OF PROPHECY

2 | BIBLICAL FOUNDATIONS OF THE PROPHETIC

A few years ago, I was speaking at a church in Northern California, and after I shared my message, I felt God telling me I needed to pray for a couple in the audience. The problem was that I didn't hear a name or know who they were. I just had an impression in my heart that there was a young couple with a business startup that needed encouragement.

I asked the Holy Spirit to give me a word of knowledge or connection to who they were. And then I was shocked by what God did (as always). I saw the name of a couple in my mind, so I asked if there was a couple by that name in the church. There was! (I am always just as thrilled as everyone else when the supernatural nature of God works in a completely normal way like this. It feels unreal, but it is *so* real.)

I told the couple another name, which sounded like the title of an organization. They seemed like they couldn't believe what was happening, and they excitedly said it was their company's name. I also told them they would be busier than bees in their next season. Everyone laughed loudly over this simple phrase, and I was not sure why (although I don't think I have ever used it before).

The audience was laughing because the young couple are beekeepers, and that was the business they were actively starting. There were other details that were helpful to their faith and journey, and even to their family. Through hearing from the Holy Spirit, I gave them a word that became a faith builder and then a blueprint for their lives.

Their company had all the markings of a successful startup, but a year later their property burned down and they lost all their hives. They had to stand in faith for their family and company, because the insurance wasn't covering all the bases. This courageous couple only had the promises of God to lean on, including my word for them, which was so specific. It put inside of them the grit and tenacity to really believe to start over.

I spent a moment with them recently and got to hear the update on their lives and business. It's been a radical journey of faith, and I was amazed at the ingenuity God had given them to solve some big problems—without the capital they used to have.

I love hearing from God. I love how it changes our options, confirms the best—and even some seemingly random—things about us, and creates a new operating system in our lives. His voice sets us on adventures we wouldn't have chosen, creates options we wouldn't have had, and helps us to fight when we face adversity.

Nothing in our Christian experience is quite as wonderful as getting to know God and hearing His heart in real time. The God of all the universe wired us on an intellectual, neurological, biological, emotional and, of course, spiritual level to hear from Him and to know Him. As we pursue Him through His Word, we will have experiences with Him. These experiences always confirm His nature, His Word, and His will.

You can't separate the Word (God's eternal word, the Bible) and the Spirit (the Holy Spirit), and we are in a time when the Church is finally focusing on the two together— which make up the most dynamic pursuit in Christianity.

God is a relator. He made you for connection and His strongest desire is for relationship with you! He cares about every aspect of His creation, and through His Spirit, He is restoring His original plan and design to humanity. This can only truly happen, though, if we hear Him.

Hearing His plan for us is not just about encouraging words or words spoken from church platforms. No, there is so much more. I am absolutely convinced that He yearns to give us His plans and desires and the structure to implement them. That is why I want to take you through a biblical journey of prophetic understanding and to show you that there is an essential reason why Paul tells us to pursue the spiritual gifts, especially prophecy (see 1 Corinthians 14:1).

We have a lot of ground to cover, and my goal is to progressively build with you as we look at prophecy and the prophetic gifts. What is its origin, and what has been its developing nature through the centuries since the Early Church? Simultaneously, we will look at the macro nature of God's voice, along with the micro.

To really understand prophetic gifts and ministry and the office of prophet, we need to look at the prophets in the Bible. We are going to start with the biblical study of prophets and the gift of the office of prophet. But don't worry, this book isn't just for prophets. It's for everyone who wants to learn how to hear from God and experience His voice as a regular, planned part of their world.

This was one of the most important themes in the Scriptures and you get to understand it! Let's demystify it and bring it into your life!

ESTABLISHING THE BEGINNING

Moses was an Israelite orphan turned Pharaoh's son who ended up embracing his Hebrew identity. Moses heard powerfully from the Lord at the burning bush in the wilderness of Midian, which led him to deeper and more profound encounters with God. Moses' obedience to God's voice brought about the end of slavery for Israel, restored their identity, returned their wealth, established their religion, and predicted their promised land.

Moses was the Lord's friend and the first prophet, who became a prototype for all others. And while Abraham heard from the Lord and was called a prophet, Moses became a *friend* of God. His prophetic relationship with Yahweh was constant. (We will explore Abraham's prophetic role in a bit.)

In Numbers 11, Moses realizes the prophetic opportunity God is giving to him. He was having more than a tough day, Israel was complaining a lot, and Moses needed help.

In Numbers 11:29, Moses is contemplating his problem and arrives at a revelation from the Lord:

I wish that all the LORD's people were prophets and that the LORD would put his Spirit on them!

Moses saw that life would be so much better if everyone was a prophet and if God would put His Spirit upon them. He knew of the divine possibilities that come with the presence and voice of God. Israel could seek their own answers and miracles for their problems—and not require Moses to provide for them. They could be comforted, guided, emotionally and spiritually developed, and, best of all, self-governed. What a revelation! What a possibility!

Moses also wanted his people to experience the glorious nature of God that he was connecting to. God, indeed, revealed His glory to Moses as He shared His plans for Israel. Moses was so taken with passion for God that he wanted everyone else to have the same experience, leading, and connection to Him as well.

As Moses saw it, the sin of man in the garden separated man from God's abiding presence. Moses was experiencing this very presence in a way that was so amazing, so satisfying, that he longed for all of God's people to have the same access.

Sadly, Israel wanted nothing to do with speaking to God. They begged Moses to speak to God for them. Moses, the composer of the first five books of the Law, was presented with no other choice but to institute the Law. And because the Israelites did not have a direct connection with God, as Moses did, they related to Him through a "container"—the Ark of the Covenant, which contained the Ten Commandments. Thus, the first formal introduction of Law-abiding prophecies comes out of Exodus 20:19, when the people say to Moses, "Speak to us yourself and we will listen. But do not have God speak to us or we will die."

This would bring us to the introduction of the Law and the prophets throughout the Old Testament. Man did not want a relationship with God the way that God wanted relationship with man. Instead, they received prophets to rule over them with the moral standards of heaven.

The law of the Lord was full of divine standards: perfect behavior in action, thought, and motive. If the Law was not executed meticulously by God's children, then they would fall outside of His protection and grace.

The reason for God's first prophet was to begin to create a framework for relationship until the return of Christ: to establish the Law that would keep His people connected with God until the Messiah's coming. Humanity needed to know how to thrive in the midst of their separation with God, and He was giving them, through the law of the prophet, a way forward. They had to know, however, that the penalty of sin was true separation from Him—and death.

Obedience to God's Word or laws brought forth the abundance of life. And until Jesus could come and pay the price for humanity's sin, God's children would learn the hard way—through intermediaries, aka prophets and representatives of God.

These heavenly representatives would deliver God's will, Law, judgments, and direction. They were God-appointed spokesmen and spokeswomen put in place to govern over the people.

Now, let's go on a journey to find out who these people are!

PROPHETIC FOUNDATIONS

In order to fully understand the gift, ministry, and office of the prophetic, we are going to build a perspective together from the foundation of the Bible. In regard to prophets, we will examine their roles, modes, jobs, types of words, and qualifiers.

Biblical prophecy illuminates a healthy standard for us today only if we apply basic rules of interpretation. Grammatical context alongside historical context allows us to have spiritual context. Many people approach the Word of God searching for spiritual context but haven't taken the time to study the Bible in a way that creates a full narrative or theology.

It's critical to remember that the entire Bible—both the Old and New Testaments—are one continuous story, all pointing to Christ. The Old Testament *foretells* of Christ, and the New Testament *tells* of Him. As we study the Word, we need to take a mountaintop view, keeping in mind the time, place, and events surrounding the particular piece of scripture we are studying.

It is dangerous to simply pick a verse here and a verse there to cobble together one's theology about the prophetic. This is called proof texting and can distort or manipulate God's Word in ways that He did not intend.

So, with these important points of context in mind, let's learn about prophecy in the Bible so that when we apply it to our lives, we will have clarity and confidence!

DEFINING PROPHECY

The next step before we go fully into the role of prophets in the Bible is to define prophecy. All through history God has been speaking to His Church. But since we all come from different backgrounds and exposures to prophecy, I am going to try to take a thoroughly inclusive approach.

Historically, prophecy has taken on many forms. God has used the prophetic realm to:

1. help create laws;

2. guide His people;

3. establish an instantaneous connection with a person and their destiny;

4. forecast for a nation;

5. call forth a home for someone in need;

6. find the lost;

7. appoint kings;

8. build wealth;

9. and provide directional insight, among many other applications.

Over the last twenty-plus years, I have trained and equipped tens of thousands in multiple aspects of hearing God's voice. While I certainly don't claim to be the leading expert, I do think my own story is unique because I have pursued these gifts and now have tons of real-life experience. I do want to point out that my experience, as extensive as it is, is only a limited version of what is possible. All of us see through a glass darkly, as it says in 1 Corinthians 13:12.

As I mentioned in chapter 1, my favorite prophetic mentor was Bob Jones, a prophet from Arkansas. One of my favorite things about Bob was how childlike he was in his curiosity toward Christianity and his experience. He never felt like he had arrived but was as hungry as a freshman Bible school student. He was always finding new ways to look at Scripture as well as the prophetic words and revelation God gave to him.

Bob was such a healthy role model for me as I grew in my own prophetic journey. He used to say, "The more mature you get, the less you feel like you know, and the bigger Papa God seems."

As much as I know, I desire to know more. As much as I experience, I want to experience more. This book is a modern model and study on a subject that definitely needs a refresh every few decades. As history advances, God is constantly bringing fresh perspective on the prophetic, and it's good to tap into the latest breakthrough thinking and current emotional intelligence on the subject.

Because prophecy at times has been a controversial subject (and not just in today's Church, but throughout history), I want to ask you a favor: suspend your caution and concern, and open up your heart and mind to some new ideas—and especially some new experiences. We have access to His voice more now than ever before in history—not because He is speaking more frequently to His children, but because we have more education and globalization of thought in Christianity.

So, what is prophecy?

Simply put: Prophecy is a divine spoken word that comes to us by revelation. God's plans and heart are revealed for a person, place, or situation.

On a deeper note, we start to see that all truth or revelation is prophetic. Prophecy is the standard of truth made available by God. Prophecy is generally given to elicit some type of specific response either by the giver or the receiver.

As we study the Old Testament, however, most of the Hebrew prophets anticipated justice through the punishment of evil. The main focus of most of their prophecies, therefore, was on a better life for Israel (God's children). They declared the standard of truth from God and illuminated the consequences if people did not change their evil ways.

And when the future was spoken about, the short-term future was the Old Testament prophets' primary focus. They did not have everlasting solutions in place, because Jesus had not yet provided Himself. The prophets would speak about coming events to bring the fulfillment of God's intentions. Most of the prophecies directly pertaining to Jesus spoke about the future Messiah or what He would accomplish.

Looking back now, assessing the biblical prophets, we see that their primary concern was with those people who were right in front of them. It is only by God's genius that we see that the prophets were unintentionally speaking about Jesus the entire time.

As you study the Bible, you start to see the recurring theme that a prophet was a spokesman of God. They were a tool through which God's words were spoken. They were called to report the news and be a loud speaker for God.

The Greek word for prophecy (*prophēteia*) denotes two central ideas:

1. FORTHTELLING OR SPEAKING FOR GOD

   Forthtelling involves insight into the will of God; it is exhortative, sharing His inspired will for the now; it also challenges believers to obey.

   In the Old Testament, it was the idea behind knowing the seasons and times that the people and/or nation of Israel were in. This required and came with foresight into God's current plans and was predictive in nature.

2. FORETELLING IS THE PREDICTION OR FORECASTING OF PRESENT AND FUTURE EVENTS

In the process of proclaiming God's message, the prophet would sometimes reveal that which pertained to the future. Interestingly, this only accounted for a small part of the prophet's message.

When we talk about the word "prophecy" that we use in modern times, we need to understand both of these uses—forthtelling and foretelling—because the gift can be used for the now or for the future.

There is an overlap in all the spiritual gifts, but it's good to note that past and present knowledge or information (and context) come from words of knowledge, which we will touch on later on in this book. (Briefly, a word of knowledge is when God provides specific, personal information that edifies or instructs another person or organization.)

When you think about prophecy, think in terms of God's will and agenda in a present and future context. In other words, it goes beyond just a single fact or word of knowledge but points to His plans, purposes and insight.

A LOOK AT THE PROPHET

A prophet in the Bible was simply someone who revealed God's messages to others. After reviewing Scripture, we define here a few key words that all refer to what we call a prophet. These words have functions and even flow attached to them, and each reveals a different view of what it means to be a prophet.

Key Prophetic Words

Nabi'—The Hebrew word *nabi'* is always translated as "prophet." This word is used not only to describe Abraham but also (in many contexts) the working of prophecy. It describes one who opens His mouth under divine direction of God; and when such a person does open his or her mouth, the Lord speaks through him or her. In other words, they often don't know what they are going to say, but the Lord speaks through their mouth when they open it.

In Genesis 20:6-7, a heathen prince named Abimelech has taken Abraham's wife, and God commands him to restore her. Speaking of Abraham, God tells Abimelech, "he is a prophet . . ." (the Hebrew word is *nabi'* as it is also in Arabic). *Nabi'* comes from the term *niv sefatayim*, meaning "fruit of the lips," which provides us grammatical understanding.

Naba'—The noun *nabi'* gave rise to the verb *naba'* meaning "to prophesy under influence of divine spirit," by divine frenzy, ecstasy, or in the ecstatic state. This describes people who have an encounter while prophesying or an encounter that directly leads to prophecy. In 1 Samuel 10, we see a band of prophets in a state of uncontrolled excitement prophesying with worship.

Afterward you will come to the hill of God
where the Philistine garrison is; and it shall be
as soon as you have come there to the city, that

you will meet a group of prophets coming down from the high place with harp, tambourine, flute, and a lyre before them, and they will be prophesying. Then the Spirit of the LORD will come upon you mightily, and you shall prophesy with them and be changed into another man.

—1 SAMUEL 10:5, *NASB*

Ro'eh—Seer. By connotation of the Hebrew word affiliated with it, it has to do with receiving a vision or visionary encounter and then prophesying out of this vision/encounter. In 1 Samuel 9:9, we see the prophet is called *ro'eh*, that is, "one who perceives." Alongside *ro'eh* we also see *chozeh* in similar passages. *Chozeh* is the "one who sees supernaturally, or has a vision" (2 Samuel 24:11). Samuel was also called *nabi'*.

DISCOVERING PROPHETS

The choice of word used to describe the prophet connotes either the mode or the way they received the prophecy. The word can also represent an authoritative title that gives light into their specific function. Not one word was wasted in the Bible. Regardless of the translation we use, we can still find the original grammatical definition.

In Deuteronomy 18:9-22, we see one of the best scriptural definitions of prophecy in the Old Testament. I particularly like verse 18:

... I will raise up for them a prophet like you from among their fellow Israelites, and I will put my words in his mouth. He will tell them everything I command him.

In this powerful passage, we see that:

- God will raise up the prophet. Prophets were not chosen or elected by men, and they were not permitted to inherit the title.
- God put His words in the prophets' mouths. (Not all prophecies are words, but most are.)

THE PROPHETS WERE FRIENDS OF GOD— ESPECIALLY MOSES

In Numbers, we see another great example of what the Lord's growth process looks like for a prophet. Also, we see the great invitation when trust is applied from God.

> ... he said, "Hear now My words: If there is a prophet among you, I, the Lord, shall make Myself known to him in a vision. I shall speak with him in a dream. Not so, with My servant Moses, He is faithful in all My household; With him I speak mouth to mouth."
>
> —NUMBERS 12:6-8, *NASB*

This scripture reveals a recurring biblical theme where the Lord desires friendship with His prophets and people. Moses' life is a prophetic picture of this type of relationship.

As we see throughout the Old Testament, God consistently makes Himself known to His prophets in visions, dreams, or face-to-face encounters. And the essence of prophecy is God making Himself known, sharing His heart, sharing His mind. It is truly about relationship.

I believe as we look back into the Old Testament to understand the prophetic, Moses becomes a picture for us. His relationship with the Lord goes past the traditional role of a prophet; he becomes someone whom the Lord views as a companion.

We see that Moses' faithfulness in all of God's purposes brought an increased trust from God. God did not veil Himself in speech, through parables in the night, or through symbolic visions. He spoke to Moses like we speak to our loved and trusted ones—a true picture of intimacy, intimacy made possible because of God's relationship with prophets.

HISTORICAL CONTEXT FOR PROPHECY

Biblical prophecy, or prophecy that is recorded within the 66 books of the Bible, is God's word for all time. It never changes. Because of the everlasting nature of biblical prophecies, we often don't see a time-related fulfillment indicated within God's Word. In other words, most prophecies in the Bible are not tied to specific dates; rather, they have to do with God's eternal love for His people and often point to Christ as Messiah.

> Every Scripture has been written by the Holy Spirit, the breath of God. It will empower you by its instruction and correction, giving you the strength to take the right direction and lead you deeper into the path of godliness. Then you will be God's servant, fully mature and perfectly prepared to fulfill any assignment God gives you.
>
> —2 TIMOTHY 3:16-17, *TPT*

If the prophecy given was part of God's ultimate biblical blueprint, then it certainly qualifies as a tool that the Holy Spirit will use to empower you to live a full life. As much as we can see in recorded biblical prophecy, I am convinced there are 1,000 times more that we don't see. Over 1,000 prophets are recorded or mentioned in the Bible, but not all of their prophetic words are recorded in the 66 books of the canon of Scripture.

Why is that? Simply put, God didn't see that particular prophecy as essential for instructing us about how to live out a life of full connection with Him. It doesn't meet the requirement that Paul described to Timothy in 2 Timothy 3:16. It may have been the word of the Lord for the original audience, but to us, it becomes bonus content.

For example, Enoch was recorded in Jude 14:14 as prophesying, but his works are not present in the canonized Bible. Also, God instructed Moses to call 70 elders together; when they gathered, the Lord put some of the Spirit upon the elders that rested upon Moses. The elders then went among the people and prophesied (see Numbers 11:25). Though we don't know what the elders said, God wanted us to know they prophesied, otherwise it would not be mentioned in the Bible.

Again, if there are more than 1,000 prophets mentioned in the Bible, then there were a whole lot of things prophesied that we know nothing about. How awesome would it be to read these messages that were spoken to these specific generations of God's people! Some of these were recorded in some of the earliest documents known to man, such as the Dead Sea scrolls and the apocrypha. Even though these texts are not part of the canon of Scripture, they are still valuable for our reflection.

Not every prophecy or revelation is reserved for the biblical cannon. Biblical revelation abides outside of time. It was around well before we were and will be around well after. We even see the Spirit of God portrayed as the Spirit of Revelation—this is an eternal theme, not just a temporary one.

Revelation was not created just for our Bible; God's revelatory word is alive today through the power of the Holy Spirit and the person of Jesus Christ. Both in the Bible and in our current times, God speaks to His children in order to reveal the fullness of His nature, works, and plans to humanity. We will always have the Word, who is now Jesus, who testifies of the same thing the written word does.

All other prophecy and revelation are celebrated and welcomed with the understanding that they are to be tested and proven true according to who God is in the Bible. As Paul instructs the church at Thessalonica, "Do not quench the Spirit. Do not treat prophecies with contempt but test them all; hold on to what is good, reject every kind of evil" (1 Thessalonians 5:19-22). So, we see that all prophecy spoken outside of the canon of Scripture is applied or tested with the scriptural prophetic framework.

Let's think of the biblical makeup together. In the Old Testament, we see God appointing prophets to use them as symbols and types—a shadow of God for His original audience and for all future audiences. God would make their prophecies part of the sufficiency of every good work (see 2 Corinthians 9:8).

The lives of these prophets were a declaration as well. Not only were they mouthpieces for God, but also their lives were symbols of a dimension of understanding from which we can learn. Their lives spoke of an everlasting message to everyone for all time.

Prophecy throughout all Scripture provides us with a full representation of Jesus. If we only see one passage or story, we only see in part; therefore, we would only know in part. On the other hand, when we see the entirety of all 66 books as the summation of God's story, we open ourselves to a timeless God and the Spirit of Prophecy.

Each person who took on a prophetic role was as important in *who* they were as in *what* their message was. Look with me at another example of how one of these leaders' lives prophesied as much as his words. This is amazing because it helps you to simply expound on the context of prototypes of Jesus.

PROPHECY ORIGINATES WITH THE HOLY SPIRIT

The Holy Spirit is the avenue for revelation and prophecy.

In the Old and New Testaments, the Holy Spirit permits the opportunity to prophecy, because He is the Spirit of Prophecy, or the Spirit of Revelation (see Ephesians 1:17). Prophecy does not exist without the Holy Spirit. It is by Him that the prophets were able to access the Creator, where prophecy dwells.

Through the Spirit of Prophecy, we can realize and invite God's divine nature into the now, even though it might have been first displayed thousands of years ago. Another way to think about this is that if you are practicing the gifts of the prophetic but are not plugged into the source, then you will not get very far relationally. You cannot maintain the practice of prophecy without practicing presence.

By presence, I am talking about being available for people—not just prophesying *to* them but also being *with* them. Be present. God is a God of relationship, and the Holy Spirit is the connector here on Earth who brings His people together. For us to be connected to God, we must be connected to the Holy Spirit. And if we are connected to the Holy Spirit, then we will be in relationship with His children.

It's all about showing up and showing that you care.

3 | CATEGORIES AND TYPES OF PROPHECY IN SCRIPTURE

I want to focus on the different types of prophecies in the Bible. As we study them, we will start to gain an understanding about what is relevant for today's pursuit of the prophetic. In our understanding, we will see what types of prophecies have already been categorically fulfilled.

When we see in Revelation 19:10 that all prophecy resides in Jesus, and He resides outside of time, we realize that His truth is not restricted by time but is made available to all for eternity. We then have permission to look at the historical types of prophecy, because through Jesus, they are as relevant today as they were millennia ago.

THE FIVE TYPES OF PROPHECIES

There are five main themes, or types, of prophecy that we see the different prophets declare in the Old Testament. Some of these types also are at play in the New Testament.

For simplicity's sake, we can look at the large majority of prophecies and place them in one of these categories. In particular, these categories will provide us with more understanding as it pertains to Old Testament prophecy. (We will revisit these five types of prophecy in the "Current Context" section so that we can see how to properly evaluate them today.)

1. MESSIANIC PROPHECIES: ALL PROPHECIES RELATING TO JESUS

It only takes a few minutes of reading the Old Testament prophets and history to discover that it is all about Jesus, the coming Messiah. The Old Testament is full of prophecies pertaining to the soon-coming King, the events surrounding His arrival, and what He will do when He arrives.

The messianic prophecies are the promise of deliverance and salvation to a nation desperate for a savior. Jesus was and is the great hope of all generations. Right from the beginning, after the fall in the garden, we see God speak a revelation to Eve that is a messianic promise. He tells her that out of her own womb (or lineage) a child would be born that would destroy the work of the snake (see Genesis 3:15). In other words, this is a prophecy of Christ's birth, resurrection and final victory that will ultimately destroy the works of Satan.

After the fall, we see God's plans shift in order to bring about Jesus in the flesh. Why? Because Adam and Eve had broken their covenant with God, and through the first sin, they were now in need of a savior. All messianic prophecies provided the original audience with a revelation of the nature of God and an everlasting proclamation of the Messiah's arrival.

Depending on what scholars you study, there are approximately 44 to 62 prominent prophecies about Jesus in the Old Testament. Some biblical experts put the number in the hundreds, but for the sake of this chapter, let's just focus on the ones that Christian Bible experts most universally recognize and accept.

In his insightful book *The Case for Faith*, pastor and author Lee Strobel says:

> Bible scholars tell us that nearly 300 references to 61 specific prophecies of the Messiah were fulfilled by Jesus Christ. The odds against one person fulfilling that many prophecies would be beyond all mathematical possibility. It could never happen, no matter how much time was allotted. One mathematician's estimate of those impossible odds is "one chance in a trillion, trillion, trillion, trillion, trillion, trillion, trillion, trillion, trillion, trillion, trillion, trillion, trillion, trillion." (Lee Strobel, *The Case for Faith* [Grand Rapids, MI: Zondervan, 2000], 262)

The messianic prophecies provided a divine landing strip for the arrival of Jesus. He was concealed in them, waiting to be revealed (see John 5:39). Let's look at just one messianic prophecy and its correlating fulfillment scripture:

A virgin will give birth, and he will be called Immanuel (God with us):

> *Prophecy: "Therefore the Lord himself will give you a sign: The virgin will conceive and give birth to a son, and will call him Immanuel"*

—ISAIAH 7:14

*Fulfillment: "The angel answered, 'The Holy Spir-
it will come on you, and the power of the Most
High will overshadow you. So, the holy one to
be born will be called the Son of God'"*

—LUKE 1:35

Some of the New Testament writers provided us with the divine connection that we were looking for—the written evidence that the Old Testament prophecies were being fulfilled. Think about the fact that the prophecies of the coming Messiah had been written down by a disparate collection of men, most of whom never met one another, and scattered across more than a millennium in a myriad of locations.

Hundreds of prophecies that had fulfillment have been found to directly link to Jesus. Each prophecy was literally fulfilled in His life, death, resurrection, and ascension. Because we now know about messianic prophecies, we understand the purpose for those prophetic words.

2. Law-Establishing and Law-Abiding Prophecies

The next type we want to highlight is Law-establishing and Law-abiding prophecies. These are all prophecies relating to the creation and adherence of the Law.

Let's talk about the beauty of the law of God, also known as the law of Moses. It is the Law set forth as a standard of truth from heaven to provide a clear distinction between right and wrong, a standard needed to be set to show the severity of sin and separation from God. However, the Law prophecies were given in the midst of God's judgment in order to remind His chosen people of His promises and love toward them.

If you love the law of God, you will resonate with the psalmist says in Psalm 119.

> *O how I love Your law! It is my meditation all the day. Your commandments make me wiser than my enemies, for they are ever mine. I have more insight than all my teachers, For Your testimonies are my meditation. I understand more than the aged, Because I have observed Your precepts. I have restrained my feet from every evil way, That I may keep Your word. I have not turned aside from Your ordinances, For You Yourself have taught me. How sweet are Your words to my taste! Yes, sweeter than honey to my mouth! From Your precepts I get understanding; Therefore I hate every false way.*
>
> —PSALM 119:97, *NASB*

The Law was provided from heaven and is our personal guardian (see Galatians 3:24). It is recorded and captured in 613 commandments, and includes some do's and some don'ts. Out of those commandments, the governing, Law-establishing and abiding prophecies came about.

The interesting thing about the Law is that it was and is the word of God, the same word of God that created the world we live in. Just like the word of God that was released and created the world, God released the Law and prophesied it into existence. The Law, delivered by God as the word of God, prophesied all by itself to all of humanity. Prophets partnered with the words that were given and prophesied to provide governance within the standard of truth.

If we see that the Law was part of God's original plan, then we start to understand how Jesus fulfilled it. We start to see the role of the Old Testament prophets all the way up to John the Baptist, who is sometimes referred to as "the hinge of history," providing a "swinging door" between the Old Testament prophecies of the Messiah and the coming of Jesus Himself. John was the forerunner, prophesying of Jesus' imminent return.

In this context, it is beautiful to see what is possible within the Law, and we start to see that it is part of God's goodness. Out of it we receive Jesus.

Prophets also functioned as preachers who expounded and interpreted the Law for the nation. Out of all of the different types of prophecies, the prophets spent most of their time giving Law-abiding prophecies.

Here are two examples of Law-establishing and abiding prophecies.

Turning from wicked ways

> *My people who are called by My name humble themselves and pray and seek My face and turn from their wicked ways, then I will hear from heaven, will forgive their sin and will heal their land.*

> —2 CHRONICLES 7:14

Hearing the Law of the Lord

> *Now go, write it on a tablet before them and inscribe it on a scroll, that it may serve in the time to come as a witness forever. For this is a rebellious people, false sons, sons who refuse to listen to the instruction of the Lord.*

> —ISAIAH 30:8-9, *NASB*

Nearly all Law-establishing and abiding prophecies were delivered in the first 39 books of the Bible. We know this because the Law and the prophets prophesied until John. Jesus brought a more perfect solution to the Law; He satisfied all of its demands. The Law was later written on our minds and in our hearts by God (see Hebrews 8:10). When this took place, it restored the relationship that God had with His people.

Present day Law-abiding prophecies are not available to give; instead we have the written Word, which becomes our text for these prophecies. There will always be confused people who try to establish new law-abiding prophecies.

When they come up with these laws, however, they are basically saying that there needs to be another work from Jesus on the cross and that what He did through His death and resurrection has not fulfilled the Law. This is patently false. We now recognize that Jesus is the fulfillment of the law.

3. Purpose and Potential Prophecies

Purpose and potential prophecies are all prophecies related to one's purpose, destiny, dreams, and capabilities; they are strengthening, encouraging, and comforting.

It is my belief that the prophets in the Old Testament spent a good amount of time trying to keep God's "stiffnecked people" from destroying themselves (and each other). So much so that the prophets simply did not have the time to prophesy regarding purpose and potential as much as the first two types of prophecy we have reviewed thus far. Nevertheless, in a lot of ways, we see some overlap within these types of prophecies.

Purpose and potential prophetic words bring forth a realization and actualization of a divine reality into someone's life. Purpose and potential prophecies are the destiny words—dreams spoken into existence through prophecy. They are the capabilities of someone's life made known and brought forth.

We will spend more time thoroughly looking at these kinds of words in later chapters. Let's look at three verses where biblical potential and purpose words were brought forth.

Restoration in Job

> Then Joseph said to him, "This is the interpretation of it: the three branches are three days; within three more days Pharaoh will lift up your head and restore you to your office; and you will put Pharaoh's cup into his hand according to your former custom when you were his cupbearer."
>
> —GENESIS 40:12-13, *NASB*

Secrets of Their Hearts Laid Bare

> But if an unbeliever or an inquirer comes in while everyone is prophesying, they are convicted of sin and are brought under judgment by all, as the secrets of their hearts are laid bare. So, they will fall down and worship God, exclaiming, "God is really among you!"
>
> —1 CORINTHIANS 14:24-25

Personal Ministry and Appointing

> As they were going down to the edge of the city, Samuel said to Saul, "Say to the servant

that he might go ahead of us and pass on, but
you remain standing now, that I may proclaim
the word of God to you."

—1 SAMUEL 9:27, *NASB*

4. BUILDING THE BODY OF CHRIST PROPHECIES

Building up the body of Christ prophecies are their own category. These are prophecies that bring corporate unification to a city or region, edify the Church, or encourage the governing body. With this type of prophecy, God speaks to establish His will in a clearer way that actually creates strategy, planning, foundation in organizations, and structure within Christian activities or bodies.

But the one who prophesies speaks to people
for their strengthening, encouraging and com-
fort. Anyone who speaks in a tongue edifies
themselves, but the one who prophesies edifies
the church.

—1 CORINTHIANS 14:3-4

Building up the body of Christ is an individual job, a community job, a church leadership job, and especially the job of Christ's appointed offices: apostles, prophets, teachers, pastors, and evangelists. Prophecies that build and unify the body of Christ can bring edification for the church on a one-to-one scale, or a governing word that changes the course of a city or nation.

The difference between the types is clear. Building the body of Christ prophecies are specific to the whole but unique enough to be for the individual. We also identify unification prophecies that better the relationship of multiple people groups. Much of the apostle Paul's writings were for the edification of the Church and included governing prophecies that brought much-needed leadership and direction.

Let's look at two different examples of these types of words in the Bible to provide us with more biblical context.

Dividing the Tribes of Israel

> *But I will take the kingdom from his son's hand and give it to you, even ten tribes. But to his son I will give one tribe, that My servant David may have a lamp always before Me in Jerusalem, the city where I have chosen for Myself to put My name. I will take you, and you shall reign over whatever you desire, and you shall be king over Israel. Then it will be, that if you listen to all that I command you and walk in My ways, and do what is right in My sight by observing My statutes and My commandments, as My servant David did, then I will be with you and build you an enduring house as I built for David, and I will give Israel to you.*
>
> —1 KINGS 11:35-38, *NASB*

Restoring Borders

> *He restored the border of Israel from the entrance of Hamath as far as the Sea of the Arabah, according to the word of the LORD, the God of Israel, which He spoke through His servant Jonah the son of Amittai, the prophet, who was of Gath-hepher.*
>
> —2 KINGS 14:25, *NASB*

5. Future-Preparedness Prophecies: Warnings, Plans, and Direction

God's Word is timeless, or outside of time. But He gives us prophecies, warnings and predictions that bring about a preparation for a soon-coming reality. As we mentioned, contrary to popular belief, future preparedness prophecies do not make up the majority of prophecies. However, they are still very important. They can help us avoid disaster in life as well as help us to navigate our lives within the context of His will.

Luke does an amazing job sharing in his Gospel how different Old Testament prophets' words were fulfilled in Jesus (e.g., Luke 1:26-31; 4:18; 22:47-48). As you are studying the Word, it is important to see that prophecy is so vast that it is not limited to one application or type. This will help you interpret what God is saying to you not just in the moment but also in the future as you ponder and reflect upon words that take on a multi-dimensional meaning.

One of the things I love about looking at future prophecies is that they are an unbelievable testament to both the nature of God and the accuracy of Scripture. No other book in the world contains fulfilled prophecies, and ours contains thousands of them! Fulfilled future prophecies validate the nature of the Word of God in a substantial way.

Let's look at two examples of biblical future-preparedness prophecy.

Cyrus Comes Forth

It is I who says of Cyrus, "He is My shepherd! And he will perform all My desire." And he de-

*clares of Jerusalem, "She will be built," And of
the temple, "Your foundation will be laid."*

—ISAIAH 44:28, *NASB*

One hundred and forty-two years later, Cyrus brought the fulfillment to this word from the book of Isaiah:

*Now in the first year of Cyrus king of Persia,
in order to fulfill the word of the LORD by the
mouth of Jeremiah, the LORD stirred up the
spirit of Cyrus king of Persia, so that he sent a
proclamation throughout all his kingdom, and
also put it in writing, saying: "Thus says Cyrus
king of Persia, 'The LORD, the God of heaven,
has given me all the kingdoms of the earth and
He has appointed me to build Him a house in
Jerusalem, which is in Judah. Whoever there is
among you of all His people, may his God be
with him! Let him go up to Jerusalem which is
in Judah and rebuild the house of the LORD, the
God of Israel; He is the God who is in Jerusalem.'"*

—EZRA 1:1-3, *NASB*

Famine in the Land

*One of them, named Agabus, stood up and
through the Spirit predicted that a severe famine would spread over the entire Roman world.
(This happened during the reign of Claudius)*

—ACTS 11:28

In a preparedness response to this prophecy about coming famine, each disciple decided to send relief. The Word
of the Lord saved a great many people:

Then the disciples, each according to his ability, determined to send relief to the brethren dwelling in Judea. This they also did, and sent it to the elders by the hands of Barnabas and Saul.

—ACTS 11:29-30

It is amazing to see this type of prophecy spread throughout the biblical generations. Clearly, God loves to create definitive markers of testimony to declare His presence. He also likes to provide plans and warnings to spare His children from calamity. God is so diverse and so are His words.

HISTORICAL DEVELOPMENT OF PROPHECY

In biblical history, prophets were regarded as more important than kings and dignitaries because they had a direct connection to God. Humanity's ability to thrive was dependent upon the connection that the prophets had with God. Nations would rise and crumble based on their ability to hear God and bring forth their words.

This is why when we look at these prophetic gifts and ministries, and office of prophet, we have to take these roles and gifts very seriously. We need to define the differences between what happened before the resurrection and what our responsibility is post-resurrection—they have a different authority structure from each other. This doesn't minimize the authority of the role or gift, but we do have to understand why there is a new dispensation and how that affects the gifts and roles of prophets.

God multiplied His voices in the days of Samuel. This is the time in Scripture when a new theme happened: the emerging of schools of prophets. Prior to the time of

Samuel, only one to perhaps a few prophets were active in each generation. And then all of a sudden, God began to hover over His people, and schools of prophets began to emerge.

Samuel not only learned God's voice, but we see through the study of history that he had the faith and ability to raise up other prophets. He trained them and released them into their ability to recognize the voice of God. We don't know what kind of exploits and missions these prophets took on, but we know by the prophets whose stories are told clearly in the Bible that there was significant purpose for all the others who were not described.

Let's look at that time in Bible history:

> *Then Saul sent messengers to take David, but when they saw the company of the prophets prophesying, with Samuel standing and presiding over them, the Spirit of God came upon the messengers of Saul; and they also prophesied.*
>
> —1 SAMUEL 19:20, *NASB*

Wave after wave of people came into the camp of Samuel and they started prophesying. The intentional, God-led inspired training that Samuel provided changed the course of history. It brought about a multiplication of the most revered and feared voices in the land.

As Isaiah 30:10 shows, the prophets brought about a perfect standard that some people did not want to hear: "They say to the seers, 'See no more visions!' and to the prophets, 'Give us no more visions of what is right! Tell us pleasant things, prophesy illusions.'"

God's voice multiplied throughout hundreds and hundreds of prophets. It was a multiplication that provided the authors, prophecies, and testimonies for numerous books of our Bible. The Bible is beautifully shaped and created by those who understood, experienced, were educated in, and practiced prophecy. It also showed that there were schools to train the prophetic voices, even in the time of Samuel, more than 1,000 years before Christ.

Hearing and speaking God's words of prophecy is a trained gift, life, and spiritual walk.

Here is an important statement that will show you why exploring the prophetic is so significant: Prophecy accounts for more than one-third of the entire Bible.

In the Old Testament, the whole of God's story plays out through the prophetic. In the New Testament, we have the manifestation of prophecy: Jesus. In the book of Acts and elsewhere in the Epistles we see how prophetic utterance also provided divine guidance in making important decisions in the early days of the spread of Christianity.

For example, in Acts 21, the disciples of Tyre were urging Paul not to go to Jerusalem for the hardships that would face him there (see v. 4). Then again, Paul had been warned "in every city" that prison and difficulties awaited him (Acts 20:23).

Prophecy in the New and Old Testaments is entirely built around the Spirit of God. When the Spirit of God would come upon someone, they were permitted to prophesy. As the creative voice of God was released in men and women, God's word was released.

There is a connection to God through His Spirit that is *always* present. It is not just a gift or an ability but also a connection to the heart or Spirit of the Creator. In later chapters we will further define the connection between God's Spirit and prophecy.

Jesus modeled this connection so well. We know He was operating out of God's Spirit, as He declared it in Luke 4:18 as He read the part of the scroll of Isaiah that prophesied of His coming. After He finished reading, He handed the scroll back to the attendant, sat down, and said, "Today this scripture is fulfilled in your hearing."

Can you imagine being in that room, hearing this man declare that He was the Messiah that Isaiah had prophesied about nearly 700 years earlier? Somehow, it's even more powerful that He sat down before He declared it; it's as if the monumental truth of it did not require Him to stand up and shout it.

In John 14 and 16, Jesus promises His disciples that the Holy Spirit would soon come to them and dwell with them (see 14:16-17; 16:7-8), and then to the Early Church as well, and all the believers in the upper room in Acts 2. He always intended on sharing His Spirit with us so that we could truly know Him. God's Spirit caused Jesus to prophesy, heal the sick, cast out demons, and give instruction.

Jesus revealed Himself to be our source.

In the next chapter, we will explore the context of prophecy for today and how Jesus remains at the center of God's prophetic plan.

4 | A CURRENT CONTEXT FOR PROPHECY

As you enter into the prophetic journey to hear God's voice, you will be confronted with people who don't believe in it, either biblically or practically. Some people will have bits and pieces of biblical teaching but without a foundation of healthy theology to support their beliefs.

Some will say that the gifts stopped operating and that prophecy was fulfilled with Jesus or the Early Church. Others will say that you can't learn these gifts or how to be prophetic because God appoints them and they are not pursuable.

It's important to look closely at the big picture and see the current context for prophecy. As you understand the culture and are hit with people who reject the idea that prophecy is still active today, you will be able to give a ready biblical answer (see Peter 3:15). As you do, you will have clear understanding and joy in the journey.

JESUS AT THE CENTER

As you read the entire Bible, you see that Christ is the center of what all prophecy is about.

In Christ, all prophecy both originates and finds its destination. When He comes on the scene in the Gospels, we see Christ fully radiating the brilliance of God and manifesting what the earlier prophets could only have reflected partially. We have not only a source of prophecy but also this source is the person of Christ Jesus. He is the one in whom all truth abides. When Jesus came to the earth, finally all past prophecy found its home in Him. Jesus then became the eternal birthing ground for all future prophecy for all of eternity.

John 1 calls Him the Word of God and says that Jesus was with God in the beginning (see John 1:1-4). He is the eternal prophetic decree to all of humanity. As such, we need to approach the Word with this depth of understanding. Because God's Word is eternal (i.e., outside *chronos*, or conventional time), it can be fulfilled historically (in the life and resurrection of Christ two millennia ago) yet still be available prophetically forever. The two facts are not mutually exclusive.

The Word can historically be fulfilled but yet still prophetically be available forever. When you look at the scriptures' fulfillment of Christ, we can create a bridge to how the gifts of God are still at work today. In other words, as prophecies from the Old Testament are fulfilled by Christ in the New Testament, it shows that it was always part of His design to reveal His nature and keep it front and center.

Those who came before us biblically became tokens (or examples) of God's nature to us. These heroes of God made it possible for us to see more fully, experience God more deeply, realize our salvation more completely, steward the kingdom more wisely, and become the fullness of Christ's reward.

When you grasp this biblical understanding, you realize that God is active and alive and speaking to His Church *now*—that humanity is perfectly situated to take hold of the nature of God and bring it forth on the earth. Who would want to limit these gifts and revelation from humanity?

The devil alone would say God's gifts and His nature are not available to us. But if we see the work of Christ from His perspective, then we see that He did everything to give us *more* access to Him today—here and now (not less access). His life was not just historical record but a fulfillment for humanity to bring forth the Spirit of Revelation forever and always.

> *Then I fell at his feet to worship him. But he said to me, "Do not do that; I am a fellow servant of yours and your brethren who hold the testimony of Jesus; worship God. For the testimony of Jesus is the spirit of prophecy."*
>
> —REVELATION 19:10, *NASB*

In this part of Revelation, John the apostle falls at the feet of an angel, and the angel quickly admonishes John to rise—to worship Jesus. This verse, where the angel says that the testimony of Jesus is the spirit of prophecy, provides us with a simplified summation describing our prophetic access to God.

The evidence and record of Jesus actively bring forth the divine, now. Everyone who has a connection to Jesus, either through a story, scripture, dream, thought, etc., has access to everything God's Spirit can provide. If you read my book *Translating God*, I teach about how Jesus' joy set before Him is His bride (His Church); this is what His heart is alive with.

Reproducing the active, life-changing nature of God within prophecy was always God's wonderful plan. How could God turn off the Spirit of revelation within Himself and restrict it with His children? Why would a loving Father want to stop communicating with His children? It is not possible; it is His Spirit to prophesy, and His nature is revelatory. As long as He is God, His Spirit will continue to prophesy.

THE SPIRIT OF PROPHECY TODAY

The Old Testament model was never God's ultimate desire for the Spirit of Prophecy. We see that in the example of Moses, whose wish was "that all the LORD's people were prophets and that the LORD would put his Spirit on them!" (Numbers 11:29)—not out of duty, but out of relationship.

We also see that Moses talked to God face to face and surpassed the normal role of leading God's people or being a spokesman. He was God's friend, which set a standard of responsibility for all other prophets who came after him (see Exodus 33:11).

I am sure everyone from Jeremiah to Ezekiel wanted the Lord to tell the world that they were His friends and not just His servants or messengers. Moses had set the bar fairly high, and they wanted what he had! Who wouldn't want God to call them friend by name!

Prophecy was the only means for this type of intimacy and friendship with God in the Old Testament. It was the highest and most sought-after commodity when people needed to communicate with God. It was sufficient for the time being, but it was not God's end game.

When we look at the contrast between Old and New Testament prophets, there are two key ingredients that make the roles very different before and after the Resurrection.

THE FIRST KEY: Jesus brought forth a very important transition in history with the Spirit of God. Through the works of Jesus, a payment for sin could be made.

Thereafter, Jesus' work fulfilled all righteousness; He atoned for our failures and missteps. This means that in the New Testament faith (or New Covenant), if a person prophesies and misses it, they can ask for forgiveness. They can take responsibility. Jesus' love covers their mistakes.

THE SECOND KEY: Jesus also provided us an abiding of His Spirit: "And with that he breathed on them and said, 'Receive the Holy Spirit'" (John 20:22). For the second time in history (the first was the Garden of Eden), God's Spirit not only *rested upon* someone for duty or His service but also *abided inside* someone other than Jesus.

Then, after Pentecost, everywhere His disciples went they released the Holy Spirit upon everyone they encountered who wanted to become connected to God through Jesus (see Acts 2).

His Spirit was given freely to the disciples and the Early Church and was now here to stay. The promised Holy Spirit was now available to rest and abide on someone in the same manner as He did with Jesus.

But even more, the Holy Spirit wasn't just limited to the disciples or someone with an official declared title from heaven (contrary to some popular theologians); rather, the Holy Spirit was available to *everyone*—and where the Spirit is, there is revelation of His nature, which is prophecy!

THE HOLY SPIRIT-PROPHECY CONNECTION

More than 45 times in the Bible God's Spirit is mentioned directly in accompaniment with prophecy. First Samuel 10:6 says, "Then the Spirit of the Lord will come upon you mightily, and you shall prophesy with them and be changed into another man" (*NASB*). The connection between the Spirit of God and prophecy is indisputable throughout the Bible, in both Testaments. If by the Spirit we receive salvation, then we too have access to prophecy by the Spirit.

In Acts 2, the disciples, now having the abiding Spirit of God, showed up in the upper room. Let's take a look at what happens:

> *When the day of Pentecost had come, they were all together in one place. And suddenly there came from heaven a noise like a violent rushing wind, and it filled the whole house where they were sitting. And there appeared to them tongues as of fire distributing themselves, and they rested on each one of them. And they were all filled with the Holy Spirit and began to speak with other tongues, as the Spirit was giving them utterance. Now there were Jews living in Jerusalem, devout men from every nation under heaven. And when this sound occurred,*

the crowd came together, and were bewildered because each one of them was hearing them speak in his own language. They were amazed and astonished, saying, "Why, are not all these who are speaking Galileans?"

"And how is it that we each hear them in our own language to which we were born?"

"Parthians and Medes and Elamites, and residents of Mesopotamia, Judea and Cappadocia, Pontus and Asia, Phrygia and Pamphylia, Egypt and the districts of Libya around Cyrene, and visitors from Rome, both Jews and proselytes, Cretans and Arabs—we hear them in our own tongues speaking of the mighty deeds of God."

And they all continued in amazement and great perplexity, saying to one another, "What does this mean?" But others were mocking and saying, "They are full of sweet wine."

Then Peter stood up with the Eleven, raised his voice and addressed the crowd: "Fellow Jews and all of you who live in Jerusalem, let me explain this to you; listen carefully to what I say. These people are not drunk, as you suppose. It's only nine in the morning! No, this is what was spoken by the prophet Joel: 'In the last days, God says, I will pour out my Spirit on all people. Your sons and daughters will prophesy, your young men will see visions, your old men will dream dreams. Even on my servants, both men and women, I will pour out my Spirit in those days, and they will prophesy. I will show wonders in the heavens above and signs on the earth below, blood and fire and billows of smoke. The sun will be turned to darkness and the moon to blood before the coming of the great and glorious day of the Lord. And everyone who calls on the name of the Lord will be saved.'"

—ACTS 2:1-21, *NASB*

PROPHECY IS ON DISPLAY EVEN MORE THAN TONGUES

In Acts 2, God's Spirit was poured out and filled the whole house. The disciples started prophesying to each other—in each others' languages! They were speaking forth the purpose and potential words of God in a foreign dialect. They spoke directly to each other with amazement and great perplexity. Their hearts were made bare and everything for them was changed in that moment.

So powerful!

Note that *everyone* there was filled with the Spirit of God. I should add, however, that the Bible makes no reference to every one of these people being prophets (i.e., not everyone was seated in the office of prophet). Of course, this is very different from the Old Testament, when prophesying was generally reserved for prophets.

Once Jesus came, and after Pentecost, prophecy became an everlasting gift given to humanity as a byproduct of the filling of the Holy Spirit! This helps also build a bridge to better understand why Paul would encourage everyone to pursue it. It was part of the atonement and part of the release of what the Early Church focused on; it was also part of the promise of Jesus when He said we would have the Holy Spirit.

Everything changed in that moment.

The Holy Spirit was released upon every willing person. What could limit the Holy Spirit now?

The first generation of Christians received the Holy Spirit, and so too can we. The Holy Spirit makes His gifts available to everyone at any time. As Hebrews 13:8 says, Jesus is the same yesterday, today, and tomorrow. If Jesus brings the Spirit of prophecy and is unchanging, then why would our access to prophecy change and not be available today? Aren't the gifts just as accessible today as they were a mere 2,000 years ago—which, to God, is simply the blink of an eye?

The theological underpinnings of the gifts are not restricted to a cessation. In other words, why would God cease our access to a gift that He says should be sought above all other gifts of the Spirit (see 1 Corinthians 14:1)? It makes no sense.

Time cannot stop the Holy Spirit. He lives outside of it.

Welcome to our current context! It's such an exciting time in history, where the Spirit of God provides the sufficiency of heaven to those in whom He abides and upon whom He rests. God knew that this power, access, and relationship with the prophetic would be more than an incredible gift to humanity—it would be His original plan restored.

The Lord also knew that in order to grow and maintain what He was building, He needed to provide a healthy structure for His people to be trained up and empowered. He set up the prophetic gifts, ministry, and office to help equip people to live their full calling. They are incredible gifts that help the body of Christ to be built up strong so that, as Paul says, they may attain "the whole measure of the fullness of Christ" (Ephesians 4:13).

God's desire to be intimately involved in our daily lives is evident in the prophetic gift. This gift is far beyond—and better than—what most would think or imagine. Through the Spirit of God (which is the Spirit of Prophecy), a person/messenger can hear from God about another person, place, or situation, from any God-known detail. Essentially, what God knows becomes available to us, in order to bring forth the reward of Jesus on the earth.

BIG-PICTURE GOALS

Prophecy is the chosen gateway of heaven for us to reveal God's nature to the world in all things, including every situation, occupation, and person. The impact of prophecy is holistic across humanity, the opportunities, macro decisions in our life, all the way down to the intricacies of our desires.

Paul and the early Christians heard God and obeyed what He said, and it caused an exponential explosion of growth that no other model or structure could have brought. Their church-planting plan was simple: hear and obey.

> These are the things God has revealed to us by his Spirit. The Spirit searches all things, even the deep things of God. For who knows a person's thoughts except their own spirit within them? In the same way no one knows the thoughts of God except the Spirit of God. What we have received is not the spirit of the world, but the Spirit who is from God, so that we may understand what God has freely given us.
>
> —1 CORINTHIANS 2:10-12

In the big picture, we start to see that God has an agenda over everything. What is more amazing is that He wants our partnership in realizing that agenda. The Lord wants to use us to help Him reapply His original design and pattern so that we can enter into the fullness of His beautiful plan. When we align our lives to His plans, we start to see His heart in all areas and spheres of authority: justice issues, industries and commercial purposes, politics through regions, countries, people groups, etc.

Through the life of Jesus, we have access to the spirit of prophecy, and in Him we find the desires of His heart. In the New Testament, we see that God promised Jesus that His reward would be a fully restored relationship to us through His sacrifice. One of prophecy's main goals has now become to restore God's original design so that we can be worthy of the price Jesus paid.

Our Father wants us to see everything the way that He intended it and to approach it through the eyes and hearts of a prophetic culture—to call forth His purposes that are not yet developed as though they are. This is how we partner in giving Jesus His reward—we call it forth.

WHAT IS THE REWARD OF JESUS?

The reward of Jesus is His eternal promise and plan on the earth for everyone. It is Christ's desires manifested on the earth in each and every one of us. All of the promises of the kingdom constitute the reward of Jesus. The following is a consolidated list of His rewards so that you can prophesy accordingly:

- We are the joy that has been set before Him (see Hebrews 12:2).

- He will do anything to have deep communion and relationship with us (see Revelation 3:20; Luke 15:3-7).
- His rewards include the fullness of salvation, spirit, soul, body, and mind (see Ephesians 3:19).
- Christ's power brings any redemptive purpose on the earth needed to reverse the effects of sin (see Romans 8:2).
- His Spirit will renew our mind and replace the carnal mind (see Romans 12:2).
- He desires to prosper His people (see Jeremiah 29:11).
- Jesus provides everyone with fruitfulness in every area of life (see John 15:1-27; 2 Peter 1:5-9).
- He is establishing God's kingdom on the earth (see Psalm 23).
- Using us as His vessels, He is creating a dwelling place for Christ, in all of the mountaintops and spheres of society (see Ephesians 3:14-17).

This provides us with the ultimate context for God's will on the earth, here and now: to see Christ glorified, the lost saved, and the earth transformed by His Spirit and power. The reward of Jesus is our opportunity to partner with God and provide Him with the reward He is due. Jesus gave His life for us, and the fruit of our lives becomes His heavenly reward.

Thoroughly study the kingdom and the byproducts of Jesus' actions. This will show you God's desires for today. Our everlasting salvation is only one reason why Christ gave His life on the cross. Jesus paid a tremendous price so that He could build His Father's kingdom along with us.

Jesus is asking us to partner with God so that God's will in heaven will be done on the earth. This is the greatest opportunity that has ever been given to any race, any people, at any time.

A partnership with God. Amazing!

I love what Paul says to the believers at Corinth about this intimate collaboration:

> *For we are partners working together for God, and you are God's field. You are also God's building. Using the gift that God gave me, I did the work of an expert builder and laid the foundation, and someone else is building on it. But each of you must be careful how you build. For God has already placed Jesus Christ as the one and only foundation, and no other foundation can be laid.*
>
> —1 CORINTHIANS 3:9-11, *GNB*

We get to co-labor with heaven so that Jesus will get His full reward! There must be a transfer, however, of cognitive understanding into experiential practice. As we move into the next few chapters, our goal will be to help you activate these prophetic gifts in your life.

Remember: God wants to partner with *you* to help bring forth heaven on Earth today!

Jesus taught us how to pray through what we now call the Lord's Prayer. This prayer is not a distant prayer that Jesus modeled for us. It is a here and now prayer. I want to close this chapter with the prayer. As I do, breathe it in;

let it be a prophetic prayer for you and your life, and listen as the Lord whispers back to you, His co-laborer in Christ.

> *Our Father, which art in heaven, hallowed be thy Name, thy kingdom come, thy will be done,* on earth as it is in heaven. *Give us this day our daily bread. And forgive us our trespasses, as we for-give those who trespass against us. And lead us not into temptation, but deliver us from evil.*
>
> —MATTHEW 6:9-13, *KJV*

5 | THE STRUCTURE OF SPIRITUAL GIFTS

If you are like me, you like structure. I love when I can pick up tools and a plan and get to work on building something beautiful.

Thank God that He built with a beautiful order: Before Jesus ascended to heaven, He gave very clear instructions to His followers. He told them to wait for the gift God had promised, which was that Christ's followers would be baptized not in water but in the Holy Spirit (see Acts 1:4-5).

While Jesus was still with His disciples, He encouraged them by saying that the Spirit would come upon them, and that they would be filled with power. And even more, that they would be His messengers even to the most remote places on Earth (see Acts 1:8). He released the Spirit of God to empower ministries that would build His kingdom and in powerful ways that would transform the world. And that empowerment is still active and alive today.

In order to fully realize God's plan on Earth through His Church, Christ brought us the fivefold ministries. I want to identify these five roles as gifts from Christ Jesus Himself to help build His government on the earth. He would never give us such a big mandate as building His kingdom without giving us the tools to do so.

The five gifts, as detailed by Paul in Ephesians 4:11, are the gifts of apostle, prophet, evangelist, pastor, and teacher. These gifts are intended for the Church to help bring governance and order to His kingdom works on Earth.

Though these roles were present throughout the entire Bible, after Christ came they were established as His plan. They would provide the heavenly structure that was needed to effectively distribute and administer God's will in the now:

> So Christ himself gave the apostles, the prophets, the evangelists, the pastors and teachers, to equip his people for works of service, so that the body of Christ may be built up until we all reach unity in the faith and in the knowledge of the Son of God and become mature, attaining to the whole measure of the fullness of Christ. Then we will no longer be infants, tossed back and forth by the waves, and blown here and there by every wind of teaching and by the cunning and craftiness of people in their deceitful scheming. Instead, speaking the truth in love, we will grow to become in every respect the mature body of him who is the head, that is, Christ. From him the whole body, joined and held together by every supporting ligament,

grows and builds itself up in love, as each part does its work.

—EPHESIANS 4:11-16

Christ gifts us the personnel, the players in their specific roles, which are the apostles, prophets, evangelists, pastors, and teachers. They are the ultimate servants of all. While some may teach, not all are seated in the office of teacher. And likewise, while God encourages everyone to prophesy, not everyone is seated in the office of the prophet.

HOW DOES PROPHECY WORK?

By a prophet the LORD brought Israel out of Egypt, and by a prophet he was preserved.

—HOSEA 12:13, *NKJV*

In God, an *original* design resides—a more perfect us, physically, emotionally, situationally, relationalonally, financially, and spiritually. God desires for us to first know about it. He shares His heart and mind with us in various ways. As we begin to see what is possible through prophecy, we become what He originally intended.

HEARING THE MASTER'S VOICE

What is in the heart of God is made possible through His voice. An awesome thing about God's voice is that His children recognize it: "My sheep hear My voice, and I know them, and they follow Me"

—JOHN 10:27, *NKJV*

And in one moment, a whisper of God's voice can bring forth a correction to a life lived in disarray or enrich one that already lives for Him. All revelation always has a source and focal point.

By inviting God's voice to guide and direct us, we open ourselves to His realities, possibilities, and opportunities. As we listen to the Shepherd, we invite Him to direct our steps and are able to live a supernatural life—rather than be confined to our old natural one. And when the most powerful conductor of change (God's Word) is channeled through prophecy, it has endless possibilities.

The Holy Spirit, coupled with a willing person to host Him, brings forth the gifts and especially the gift of prophecy. A willing vessel is one whom God has chosen (and we are all chosen; see 1 Corinthians 14:31).

As we submit ourselves to Him, we will grow in our ability to receive the now-present word of the Lord concerning a person, place, or situation. And the giver delivers the word in its proper setting to the receiver, and the receiver is exposed to greater opportunities in every aspect of their lives.

There is the subject and object of the revelation, but behind the revelation itself is the connection from which it comes: the Spirit of Jesus. Everything that God shows us is for the benefit of building Jesus' nature in the world. His revelation helps us establish Jesus' dominion, love, strength, and transformation so that He can one day inherit His great reward.

Jesus, like us, has a destiny. He paid the price on the cross to re-create our connection to His Father—which built a bridge of grace allowing us access to His salvation. As well, through Christ's death and resurrection, He has defeated Satan; His victory will lead to the restoration of

God's full, glorious plan—as if it had never been diverted or degraded.

Jesus' triumph means that until He returns, our entire life's goal and pursuit is not about our destiny first or our purpose. We are called to a higher purpose than personal gain, and it is no longer our primary goal. Yes, we see beyond the passing pursuits of this world now, for we are indebted to Jesus for what He did on the cross by restoring us to the Father (see 2 Timothy 1:9).

All prophetic revelation that we receive is not centered on building our life or our world but on building His life in others and His government and power. If we gain earthly influence and power, it is so that we can serve His purposes. That is what I meant earlier when I said we have been called out of a natural existence and into a supernatural one.

Prophecy, therefore, serves as God's divine communications service, and we have been given free calling plans that allow us to receive messages from the ultimate Caller. The purpose is to promote His gifts of grace, encouragement, and salvation as we listen attentively for the Caller's voice. The more we use this service, the better we discern His voice.

As we have noted, the Bible tells us to pursue the gifts, but above all, prophecy. But understanding why we have been given this gift by the Father is critically important. When we pursue the revelatory gifts (i.e., words of knowledge and wisdom), we always have to prioritize Jesus as the focus.

If this is the foundation of your heart when you prophesy, then you will always have the right priority and connection to Jesus. You can tell when people are using discernment to build their own agenda, because you can't find Jesus in the center of it. He is either not present or off to the side of the primary agenda.

THE *LOGOS* AND THE *RHEMA*

As our loving Shepherd, God knows every single detail of our lives, past, present, and future (see Hebrews 4:13). He is determined to give us the best life now and bring forth the reward of Jesus on the earth. Does this mean we will never have trials or suffer sickness or setbacks? No. We live in a flawed and fallen world. What it does mean, however, is that He employs His creation (us) in a state of partnership and issues His voice to everyone, saved and unsaved.

Yes, that's right! We have the Word of God, but God continues to speak:

1. We have the *logos* word of God. *Logos* refers principally to the total inspired Word of God, the Bible.

2. We have the *rhema* word of God. The *rhema* is the revealed word of God, as an utterance from God to the heart of the receiver via the Holy Spirit, as in John 14:26.

> *But the Comforter, who is the Holy Ghost whom the Father will send in My name, He shall teach you all things and bring all things to your re-membrance, whatsoever I have said unto you.*
>
> —JOHN 14:26, *KJ21*

We have the written *logos* and spoken *rhema* word of God, presented to us by the Holy Spirit. In other words, we have our Bible to pattern our lives after, and we have the active voice of God to help our lives thrive.

This is where prophecy comes from: the word (*logos*) and voice (*rhema*) of God. Since the closing of the biblical canon (the 66 books of the Bible), God's partnership with us through prophecy is no longer a matter of establishing the *logos*. We have the fullness of the Word of God to live from. Prophecy today is not a matter of establishing or changing the Word of God. It is already established.

Prophecy today is built around the inspired word of God utilizing *both* the *logos* and the *rhema* word of God. Why are both so important? Simply put, God's will is clearly defined in the most beautiful way through Scripture. And His present-day active voice brings us natural and spiritual context of Scripture.

If one were to remove the *rhema* word of God from their life and only apply the *logos*, then they would be living solely out of principles (no active voice). On the other hand, if one were to remove the *logos* word of God from their life and only live out of the *rhema*, then they would have no foundation upon which to hear the voice of God.

We need both.

That is why God gave us both.

WHERE DOES PROPHECY WORK?

I have also spoken by the prophets, and have multiplied visions; I have given symbols through the witness of the prophets.

—HOSEA 12:10, *NKJV*

We have built a solid historical context for the different kinds of prophecies and our current access to prophecy. We are not limited in our understanding to what this gift currently offers us. We can identify the prophets in the Old and New Testaments, and we can relate to their unique assignments on the earth.

For some biblical prophets, such as Moses, it was to establish the word of God; for others, such as Samuel and Isaiah, it was to bring forth God's heart and mind. In other words, the Bible gives us context to what is available rather than what is unavailable. It is more of an invitation into possibility than a restriction of life.

Prophecy's only limitation is the extent to where God's voice can go. In fact, there are no boundaries, no limits, no restrictions. Prophecy is essentially the delivery of His voice, and the Church is home base for His prophetic deliveries.

God's community-church setting is a safe place to grow in all of the gifts, to steward the gifts, and to distribute the gifts. But that is not the only place in which God operates. The Spirit of God has always wanted to make its way outside of the four walls of the local church.

Then he brought me back to the door of the house; and behold, water was flowing from under the threshold of the house toward the east, for the house faced east. And the water was flowing down from under, from the right side of the house, from south of the altar.

—EZEKIEL 47:1, *NASB*

God's Spirit was flowing eastward under the threshold of the house. It could not be contained and was literally flowing out of the house that Ezekiel saw in his vision. And today, that is what God wants to do with the Church—release prophecy outside the walls of the Church. God wants the kingdoms of this world to be saturated and changed by prophecy.

We need to see where prophecy can go and be God's conduits to take it across the earth. He wants His voice to transform and redeem people everywhere.

THE KINGDOMS OF THIS WORLD

Before Jesus began His earthly ministry, the devil met with Jesus and offered Him the kingdoms of this world.

> *Again, the devil took Him up on an exceedingly high mountain, and showed Him all the kingdoms of the world and their glory. And he said to Him, "All these things I will give You if You will fall down and worship me." Then Jesus said to him, "Away with you, Satan! For it is written, 'You shall worship the Lord your God, and Him only you shall serve.'"*
>
> —MATTHEW 4:8-10, *NKJV*

The context for this verse starts in the Garden of Eden when the devil deceived Adam and Eve and took away the keys to the kingdoms of this world. Jesus came back to conquer sin, death, and the grave, and to restore the kingdoms of this world back to God and His children.

After Jesus rose victorious over sin and the devil, He received those keys back. Through Christ's perfect plan, He gave those keys back to His kids—His Church.

In Matthew 16:19, He tells Peter that He is giving His children the power and authority of the kingdom, with a direct connection to heaven.

I will give you the keys of the kingdom of heaven; and whatever you bind on earth shall have been bound in heaven, and whatever you loose on earth shall have been loosed in heaven.

—MATTHEW 16:19, *NASB*

God's interest in the kingdoms of this world, however, is not just about salvation and going to heaven. The kingdoms of this world are the spheres of society where God desires to sit on the mountaintops. The Lord desires to reign over every high place in our world and in our mind. And He wants us to use the keys of authority that we have been given and rule and reign with Christ Jesus on every mountain top.

This is where prophecy can go.

This is where God *wants* prophecy to go.

In other words, the kingdoms of this world are our oyster. They are where God wants His voice and prophecy to go.

There is a divine purpose in the distribution of God's gifts. He did not give them out just for fun. He has a plan and a purpose that He wants us to partner with Him. His plan is to invade the kingdoms of this world with the love of God and transform them into His image.

One of your best tools to do so is prophecy.

Then the Lord reached out his hand and touched my mouth and said to me, "I have put my words in your mouth. See, today I appoint you over nations and kingdoms to uproot and tear down, to destroy and overthrow, to build and to plant."

—JEREMIAH 1:5-10

God is seeking every people group, in every nation, in every occupation, in every sector of society, and in every demographic. He desires every single person in the church, home, workplace, government, entertainment, and the arts to return to Him.

Where you are today is a perfect place for prophecy to be. It's not just limited to a church or person or pulpit. Jesus did not say to just go to your small group or church. He said,

> *"Go into all the world and proclaim the gospel to the whole creation"*
>
> —MARK 16:15, *ESV*

Prophecy was always intended to go everywhere!

This is not a new concept for prophecy to go outside of the church. Statistically speaking, today only 2 percent of the population will ever be called to full-time ministry inside the church. Furthermore, most biblical prophets were called into different areas of life outside of the church. Only a few were specifically called to the church. Here are some examples of those who prophesied inside and outside of the church. They are what I call multiple-job prophets:

- Ezekiel and Jeremiah were priests as well as prophets.
- David was first a shepherd, then a warrior, king, poet, and prophet.
- Moses was a law giver.
- Solomon was a king.
- Noah was a builder.
- Amos was a herdsman (see Amos 1:1).

- Elisha was a plowman (see 1 Kings 19:15-21).
- Daniel was a government administrator (see Daniel 2:48).
- Paul was a tentmaker.
- Jesus was a carpenter.

Prophecy has no limitations, no bounds. It comes from the Creator of all things and is intended for all things. God wants His voice to infiltrate every area of society.

Will you take His voice into every area and sphere of your life?

GOD'S BIG-PICTURE GOALS OF PROPHECY

Love

The construct of our humanity is built on the nonnegotiable reality that God created everything we know, see, and experience with love. Love is the most important force we have access to. God defines Himself as being love. Nothing motivates God like love does.

The Father's nature is hardwired to love. To some, love may just be a feeling, emotion or confession; but to God, it is the eternal power that creates and sustains entire universes. According to God, nothing meaningful starts or ends without love (see 1 John 4:7-8,19).

The goals and objectives of prophecy are built upon a framework of what we understand to be true historically and spiritually in the heart, mind, and nature of God. We have a blueprint for our prophetic gift, and His name is Jesus. We need to see the world through His eyes, with His heart, with His mind, and apply what we know with His hands.

Love is the Father's heart and perspective in any situation. Seeing the world with the eyes of Jesus provides us with a lens of love. Because God is love.

The true intended purpose of His voice is to bring us into a deep intimate relationship. Prophecy is a communicated extension of love. Love is also the prerequisite of prophecy (see 1 Corinthians 13:1-2; 14:1).

Within Scripture we find absolutes, or hinges—a defined reality that creates a focal point or reference in which everything is built on, scriptures that set a precedent for everything else. Within 1 Corinthians 13, we see some scriptural hinges that perfect our understanding of prophecy. If we can master the art of love, then prophecy will come very easily to us.

Read 1 Corinthians 13 with me:

> *If I speak in the tongues of men or of angels, but do not have love, I am only a resounding gong or a clanging cymbal. If I have the gift of prophecy and can fathom all mysteries and all knowledge, and if I have a faith that can move mountains, but do not have love, I am nothing. If I give all I possess to the poor and give over my body to hardship that I may boast, but do not have love, I gain nothing. Love is patient, love is kind. It does not envy, it does not boast, it is not proud. It does not dishonor others, it is not self-seeking, it is not easily angered, it keeps no record of wrongs. Love does not delight in evil but rejoices with the truth. It always protects, always trusts, always hopes, always perseveres. Love never fails. But where there are prophecies, they will cease; where there are tongues, they will be stilled; where there is knowledge,*

it will pass away. For we know in part and we prophesy in part, but when completeness comes, what is in part disappears. When I was a child, I talked like a child, I thought like a child, I reasoned like a child. When I became a man, I put the ways of childhood behind me. For now, we see only a reflection as in a mirror; then we shall see face to face. Now I know in part; then I shall know fully, even as I am fully known. And now these three remain: faith, hope and love. But the greatest of these is love.

When Jesus spoke to the woman at the well, her confession was that she felt fully known (see John 4:4-26). That is what love does; it makes us feel fully known by God and people. We are made fully known through love.

Tools of Love

The prophetic is one of the greatest tools of love we have. Picture how technology has created a platform of connection in one generation. We can communicate virtually anywhere in the world through smart devices, Internet services, content streaming, virtual reality, and so on. Technology has created the connection for anyone to talk anywhere to any of their friends, and to even make new ones. We can become part of an online community that we would have never had access to without it.

The prophetic is meant to be like this: it is the technology or smart device to our spiritual love. It is the tool that accelerates relationship and creates connection with people, cities, countries, industries, and the world. Through it we see a very real glimpse of God's heart and get to treat people exactly the way God intended them to be treated from the beginning.

As with technology, revelation was not just meant to inspire us (in this case, with prophetic gifts) but also to help us live with a stronger, clearer connection—in this case, a better line to how God feels and what He thinks.

The prophetic path is a way of life—it allows us to see people the way God always longed for them to be seen and, from that revelation, to treat them out of His culture of love. In doing so, God uses us to help them become the version of themselves that He and we see. Having a deep relationship with God that includes authentic friendship will definitely lead you into sharing that kind of relationship and friendship with others.

Many people pursuing prophetic gifts are about as close with God as they are with their yearbook friends, but they still insist on trying to use prophecy on others. Then they get discouraged about the lack of relational depth developed through the experience. It's because prophetic ministry is about your being a gateway to God's thoughts, emotions, and heart for others through your connection to Him.

The world is full of seven-plus billion pieces of God's heart, and as you get to know Him, you begin to absorb His affection for humanity. Your relationship with Him is the primary source and goal of revelation.

THE STRUCTURE RESTORED

The prophetic structure is based on God's *logos* and *rhema* word, laid upon the foundation of His love. This structure declares the Father's mind and intention. And when we speak on God's behalf, we reveal not only *what* He says but also *who* He is.

God's intentions are made known in His *logos* and *rhema* word. If we don't know what's in God's will, then how can we steward the representation of God's gifts well? Through His Word, we are informed that we have access to the mind, heart, and will of God.

The fullness of God was brought forth through the testimony of Jesus, who is the entirety of the Word. We see God's covenant in His promise of fruitfulness with Adam, in His blessing to Abraham as a father of nations, in His promise to Noah in protecting the earth, and in His commitment to David to make him a king.

Depending upon the source, there are somewhere between 3,000 and 5,500 promises in the Bible. Our goal here is not to do an in-depth study on God's promises to His people. Rather, we want to highlight the fact that God loves us so much that He *makes* and *keeps* His promises.

Consider Abram. He's living in Ur (modern-day Iraq), growing old with his wife, Sarai, and they have no children. Suddenly, God speaks to him, gives him and his wife new names—Abraham and Sarah (see Genesis 17:5)—and says that not only will he have children but also that his descendants will be as numerous as the stars and the sand of the seashore (see Genesis 22:17).

What would you have thought of such promises if you were Abraham? Before God spoke to him, he purportedly worked with his father, Terah, making idols for pagans who worship the moon (see Joshua 24:2). Now a new God comes to you—a God called *YHWH*.

Remember, you are 86 years old when your first child is born, and 100 when your second son is born (Abraham's ages, respectively, when Ishmael and Isaac were born; see Genesis 16:1-6; 21:5).

If we are honest with ourselves, there would probably be just a seed of doubt (even for the most faithful among us). But God did indeed open Sarah's womb, and from this one couple was birthed all twelve tribes of Israel (his son Isaac gave birth to his grandson Jacob, who was the father of the leaders of the twelve tribes).

Have God's disbursement of promises ended today? Or did they cease when the apostles and disciples passed away two millennia ago? No. Through the foundation of the *logos* and the Holy Spirit's use of the *rhema*, we, His children, the spiritual descendants of Abraham, have access to the same God. His promises continue.

Now let's focus on how to bring forth God's will within His biblical promises. We need to learn how to speak out of God's promises.

> *And because of his glory and excellence, he has given us great and precious promises. These are the promises that enable you to share his divine nature.*
>
> —2 PETER 1:4, *NLT*

The prophetic can be used to bring us into:

1. THE FULLNESS OF OUR SALVATION

   God wants us to come into the fullness of our identity and our destiny. Philippians 2:12-13 (*NKJV*) says:

   > *Therefore, my beloved, as you have always obeyed, not as in my presence only, but now much more in my absence, work out your*

*own salvation with fear and trembling; for it
is God who works in you both to will and to
do for His good pleasure.*

2. THE RESTORATION OF ALL THINGS

   God wants all things to be completely restored
   to His original design. Acts 3:21 says:

   *Heaven must receive him until the time comes
   for God to restore everything, as he promised
   long ago through his holy prophets.*

3. THE ESTABLISHMENT OF GOD'S KINGDOM

   Jesus came to establish God's kingdom. Luke
   11:1-4 (*ESV*) says:

   *Now Jesus was praying in a certain place, and
   when he finished, one of his disciples said to
   him, "Lord, teach us to pray, as John taught his
   disciples." And he said to them, "When you pray,
   say: 'Father, hallowed be your name. Your kingdom come.'"*

4. THE REWARD OF JESUS

   Our Father in heaven wants to give Jesus the
   fullness of His reward. Jesus paid the ultimate
   price for our partnership and God is a strategic
   investor. He wants one heavenly return on the investment that He made in us and on Earth. God's
   investment dividend will be a perfected bride,
   without spot or blemish, with no missing teeth.
   This is what Jesus desires:

   *... for Jesus loved the church and gave himself
   up for her to make her holy, cleansing her by
   the washing with water through the word, and*

to present her to himself as a radiant church,
without stain or wrinkle or any other blemish,
but holy and blameless.

—EPHESIANS 5:25-27

5. GOD'S WILL

The entity of Scripture is God's will sufficiently presented to us. I would encourage you to study the scriptures and find yourself approved (see 2 Timothy 2:15). Discover the heart and nature of God available within the Bible.

Jesus worked relentlessly every day until the cross to bring us back into that heavenly relationship. God's integrated partnership with humanity is a display that no other religion provides: an active relationship with almighty God.

Inside the healthy structure of relationship, prophecy can thrive. But when prophecy is given outside the structure of relationship, it doesn't find a home. Through prophecy, we can embody the Word of God and share its heart, mind, will, and emotions to those around us. God doesn't want to do it without us. Even in our imperfect state, He wants to be known in us and wants us to be known.

Consider the fact that Jesus was 12 (not yet a teenager) when He was about His Father's business.

And He said to them, "Why did you seek Me?
Did you not know that I must be about My
Father's business?"

—LUKE 2:49, *NKJV*

Jesus is our perfect model. As we connect more closely with God through time spent with Him, prayer, worship, and fellowship, we will be better able to be about our Father's business.

So many things press in, wanting to disrupt God's divine structure of prophecy. Through Christ, and the guidance of the Holy Spirit, we will be able to guard our connection with God at all costs.

6 | THE BENEFITS OF PROPHECY

Why prophecy?

What are the tangibles and incentives for why anyone would even pursue this gift?

When Paul wrote to the Corinthians to eagerly desire it, he would have never made such a case if he hadn't experienced the direct benefits of prophecy firsthand.

When we hear God, we see that through the power of His intention and Spirit, mountains can be moved, nations can be saved, and the fullness of the Lord's redemptive work becomes available to us through prophecy.

Heaven's plan is laid out in 1 Corinthians 14:1:

Follow the way of love and eagerly desire [burn with zeal] gifts of the Spirit, especially prophecy.

Prophecy is one of the Spirit's best delivery methods to bring a kingdom result into our now. Through prophecy, what might take twenty life-coaching or counseling appointments might happen through one revelation. What can take years of wisdom-building through life experience can be brought to you in a moment if God shares Himself with you. When prophecy comes, it's not just words; it's the substance of God making Himself available to you.

I have personally experienced and witnessed so many of the benefits of God releasing a prophecy. One of my favorites, however, had to do with the house we now live in. The story could take up a book in itself to properly unfold the entire prophetic story.

The top line is that God made it clear—through more than forty-seven prophetic words—that He was going to help us purchase a house in Los Angeles that was out of our price range. His purpose was to give us a place that was not only great for our family but also would have a strong impact on our ministry—a gathering place for people, especially Christians working in the entertainment industry.

I had actually received prophetic words about a home in L.A. from people for more than fifteen years. But by the time I moved to California, it seemed impossible that we would ever be able to qualify for a mortgage.

Sometimes, however, the impossible is the most fertile seedbed for the prophetic—God loves to plant His words amidst circumstances *we* see as impossible. And then, when the facts on the ground tell you "no way" and then God makes a way, your faith blossoms and flourishes.

It's not like my wife, Cherie, and I lived our lives in anticipation of this house, but we kept our spirits open to the possibility. The final prophetic word about the home came from Cindy Jacobs, one of the most well-known prophets today.

Cindy said, "I see the real estate listing of a house that God wants to give you. It's a house that has had entertainment industry history, and you will make history with God there. The listing even says, 'Hollywood History Was Made Here.'"

She described the house, the other buildings on the property, the type of street it was on, and many other details. I shared the word with my wife, who had actually just been looking at houses on the market in L.A.

She shocked me when she said, "There is a listing that says that."

"Says what?" I asked.

"'Hollywood History Was Made Here' is the listing title. The property is exactly what she described."

We made an appointment to go see the house and through a series of miracles were able to purchase it! It's the house we currently live in, and many kinds of ministry and kingdom purposes have been birthed out of it.

One of the main benefits of prophecy is that it releases you from living a normal life, bearing normal man-made fruit. Instead, as you partner with God, you bear fruit that is greater than what you could otherwise accomplish in your own gifts, strengths, and abilities (or lack thereof). The prophetic life gives you a result that you couldn't earn; it causes you to have influence, opportunity, and resources that you probably wouldn't have even considered or been able to pursue.

When you hear from God, your options change. You now come directly under His spoken will and you become a direct beneficiary of the reward of faith as you walk out the journey He tells you to pursue. How wonderful is that!

BENEFITS OF PROPHECY

Let's look at some of the incentives and direct benefits of letting prophecy be part of your life, as the Bible lays them out through stories:

- Redeeming desolate inheritances/lands—Jeremiah 30:1-3: "'For I, the Lord, affirm that the time will come when I will reverse the fortunes of my people, Israel and Judah,' says the Lord. 'I will bring them back to the land I gave their ancestors and they will take possession of it once again.'"

- Reveals the nature of God (see Isaiah 9:6).

- Establishes history (see Exodus 17:14).

- Restores our livelihood (see John 10:10).

- Reveals and solves the concerns of our heart—1 Samuel 9:19 says:

- Kish said to his son Saul, "Take now with you one of the servants, and arise, go search for the donkeys." . . . "Come, and let us return, or else my father will cease to be concerned about the donkeys and will become anxious for us." He said to him, "Behold now, there is a man of God in this city, and the man is held in honor; all that he says surely comes true. . . . Now therefore, go up for you will find him at once." So they went up to the city. As they came into the city, behold, Samuel was coming out toward them to go up to the high place.

- Now a day before Saul's coming, the LORD had revealed this to Samuel, saying, "About this time tomorrow I will send you a man from the land of Benjamin, and you shall anoint him to be prince over My people Israel; and he will deliver My people from the hand of the Philistines. For I have regarded My people, because their cry has come to Me." When Samuel saw Saul, the LORD said to him, "Behold, the man of whom I spoke to you! This one shall rule over My people." Then Saul approached Samuel in the gate and said, "Please tell me where the seer's house is." Samuel answered Saul and said, "I am the seer. Go up before me to the high place, for you shall eat with me today; and in the morning I will let you go, and will tell you all that is on your mind. As for your donkeys which were lost three days ago, do not set your mind on them, for they have been found." . . . So Saul arose, and both he and Samuel went out into the street. As they were going down to the edge of the city, Samuel said to Saul, "Say to the servant that he might go ahead of us and pass on, but you remain standing now, that I may proclaim the word of God to you."

—1 SAMUEL 9:3-27, *NASB*

By the spirit of prophecy, Samuel was able to see the concerns of their hearts, communicate God's thoughts, and appoint Saul as the king. It is amazing what the benefits of prophecy offered to someone who was looking for their donkeys!

Here is a personal story of one of the benefits of prophecy:

One of the largest events where I have ever prophesied was called Azusa Now in Los Angeles, California.

During a service, I received a word of knowledge for a married couple, to the point where the Lord told me their names. They had both come to the event separately because they had decided to get a divorce (though I only learned this fact after I gave the word).

I prophesied how God had brought them together, where they had met, how much they loved each other, and how God was central to their marriage. This prophetic word convicted their hearts to the point that they decided to give their marriage another try.

Afterward, I learned that God turned their marriage around as they saw, once again, God in each other and in their choice of a lifelong partner. It created an atmosphere in which their marriage could heal.

Prophecy provides us with divine appointments, life warnings, restoration, and access to the heart and nature of God. Its benefits are truly endless.

But it's up to you to explore them!

> *Come, see a man who told me all the things*
> *that I have done; this is not the Christ, is it?*
>
> —JOHN 4:29, *NASB*

WAYS GOD SPEAKS

It's impossible to deliver the heart and mind of God to yourself and the world around you unless you first learn and apply the ways that God speaks.

Throughout Scripture, God has provided us numerous ways of hearing His voice. I would like to point out some of the more common ways and to invite you into them. Each one of the ways indicated in the section below could have an entire book (or books) dedicated to studying it. For the purpose of this book, we will highlight the more common ways and build a general frame of understanding.

For starters, God speaks in many different ways. We should not put God into a box.

Hebrews 1:1 says, "In the past God spoke to our ancestors through the prophets at many times and in various ways." Out of those many ways that God speaks, we will evaluate some of the more common scriptural ways, descriptions, and biblical examples. For your reference, my list is in no particular order.

I would also encourage you to invite these different pathways into your heart and mind as you go on this educational journey. God truly wants to speak to you in these different ways!

VISIONS

The Bible contains more than 111 references to visions. There are two different types: open and closed.

With an open vision, it is like having something right before your eyes, like a motion picture or photograph (i.e., not just in your head or imagination). Sometimes an open vision resembles a still photograph or motion clips.

The second kind of vision is a closed vision. In this case, your eyes are open or closed and you have a picture in your imagination. A closed vision can also resemble a snapshot or a picture, but it is happening in your mind.

King Nebuchadnezzar of Babylon had a closed vision, which came to him as a dream. The king said, "I had a dream that made me afraid. As I was lying in bed, the images and visions that passed through my mind terrified me" (see Daniel 4:4-37).

Did you know:

- Visions tend to be interactive. In the very first verse of Jeremiah, God engages with the prophet by name: "What do you see, Jeremiah?" Also, on the mount of Transfiguration, Jesus talks to Elijah and Moses in an open vision (see Matthew 17:1-13).

- In some visions, you can also hear what is happening or being said. Paul mentions hearing inexpressible words in one of his visions (see 2 Corinthians 12:4).

Let's review some specific purposes of visions:

- To teach spiritual truth
- To convey prophecy
- To strengthen a believer during a trial
- To reveal events that would otherwise be unknown
- To reveal the power and majesty of God and Jesus Christ
- To confirm punishment for sin
- To inform someone or a group to do God's will
- To encourage and provide hope
- To confirm a blessing or promise
- To reveal God's plan for man

Here are two examples of visions from the book of Acts:

> *He has seen in a vision a man named Ananias come in and lay his hands on him, so that he might regain his sight.*
>
> —ACTS 9:12, *NASB*

> *During the night Paul had a vision of a man of Macedonia standing and begging him, "Come over to Macedonia and help us." After Paul had seen the vision, we got ready at once to leave for Macedonia, concluding that God had called us to preach the gospel to them.*
>
> —ACTS 16:9-11

DREAMS

Dreams are just as numerous as visions in the Bible, which contains more than 105 direct references to dreams. In some ways, dreams are just like visions, but they typically occur at night.

We find one of the best definitions of a prophetic dream in Job 33:14-15:

> *For God does speak—now one way, now another—though no one perceives it. In a dream, in a vision of the night, when deep sleep falls on people as they slumber in their beds...*

God truly does beautiful things when we are sleeping. God created Eve when Adam was sleeping.

Dreams are often communicated in symbolic language—a language composed of God's image and construct, the recipient's image and construct, and their environment. It is a language that needs to be learned based on the belief systems of God and man. Ninety percent of dreams are geared for self-process, and some dreams can be literal.

I place dreams in two different categories: message dreams and symbolic dreams. They both require interpretation and they activate six different types of dreams found in the Bible:

1. INTERPRETATIVE DREAMS—"At Gibeon the Lord appeared to Solomon during the night in a dream, and God said, 'Ask for whatever you want me to give you'" (1 Kings 3:5).

2. AWAKENING DREAMS—"Then Pharaoh woke up; it had been a dream. In the morning his mind was troubled" (Genesis 41:7-8).

3. WARNING DREAMS—"And having been warned in a dream not to go back to Herod, they returned to their country by another route" (Matthew 2:12).

4. DEVELOPMENT DREAMS—"Until the time came to fulfill his dreams, the LORD tested [Joseph's character]" (Psalm 105:19).

5. DIRECTIONAL/PREDICTING DREAMS—"Then He opens the ears of men, and seals their instruction. In order to turn man from his deed, and conceal pride from man, He keeps back his soul from the Pit, and his life from perishing by the sword" (Job 33:16-18, *NKJV*).

6. SELF-PROCESSING DREAMS—"In the visions I saw while lying in bed, I looked, and there be-

fore me was a holy one, a messenger, coming down from heaven. He called in a loud voice: 'Cut down the tree and trim off its branches; strip off its leaves and scatter its fruit. Let the animals flee from under it and the birds from its branches. But let the stump and its roots, bound with iron and bronze, remain in the ground, in the grass of the field'" (Daniel 4:10-18, *NKJV*).

ANGELS

Angels are abundant in the scriptures and their application is as vast as God's Word. They are called messengers, and they deliver the will and message of heaven. There are different kinds of angelic visitations and types of angels in the Bible. We will review a few of the almost 300 direct references found in Scripture.

There are many types of angels in the Bible:

1. ANGELS OF PROTECTION—"For He shall give His angels charge over you, to keep you in all your ways" (Psalm 91:11, *NKJV*).

2. MESSENGER ANGELS—In Luke 1, God sent the angel Gabriel to Mary. Messenger angels also deliver God's revelation.

3. MINISTERING ANGELS—In 1 Kings 19, an angel appeared to Elijah and provided food and water for his journey.

4. ANGELS THAT EXECUTE GOD'S JUDGMENT (2 Kings 19:35).

5. WORSHIPING ANGELS (Revelation 5:11-12).

6. HEALING ANGELS—Healing angels at the healing pool of Bethesda, John 5.

TRANCES

When we hear the word "trance," our minds might jump to hypnotists, magicians, or illusionists. But actually, a trance is simply a dream-like state when we are awake. Though trances are rare in the Bible, they are one of the most immersive ways that God speaks. A trance is like having a live encounter without the distractions of a normal experience.

A trance is a state of profound abstraction or absorption, usually characterized by partly suspended animation with diminished or absent sensory and motor activity. God can use a trance as a way of communicating without distractions.

Here are two scriptural references to trances:

But Peter began speaking and proceeded to explain to them in orderly sequence, saying, "I was in the city of Joppa praying; and in a trance I saw a vision, an object coming down like a great sheet lowered by four corners from the sky; and it came right down to me."

—ACTS 11:4-5, *NASB*

About noon the following day as they were on their journey and approaching the city, Peter went up on the roof to pray. He became hungry and wanted something to eat, and while the meal was being prepared, he fell into a trance. He saw heaven opened and something like a large sheet being let down to earth by its four corners.

—ACTS 10:9-11

IMPRESSIONS

Impressions are one of the more common ways in which people hear God.

Impressions and puns are seen throughout the Bible and are used by the Holy Spirit to nudge someone to interact with the world around them. God-inspired impressions can guide a person in ways they wouldn't have without the leading of the Holy Spirit.

Impressions often feel like a thought that is inspired, like when someone or something drops into your spirit and your empathy or feelings become heightened. Or it is when a scripture suddenly comes alive and you have a clear or new understanding of its significance for your life, a current situation, or a person. You might say, "I have read that passage thirty times, but suddenly it has deep meaning for me." Prophetic impressions are not always a "third heaven" type of dramatic experience; they are often very subtle or gentle.

Mark 2:8-12 is an example of a prophetic impression:

Immediately Jesus knew in his spirit that this was what they were thinking in their hearts, and he said to them, "Why are you thinking these things? Which is easier: to say to this paralyzed man, 'Your sins are forgiven,' or to say, 'Get up, take your mat and walk'? But I want you to know that the Son of Man has authority on earth to forgive sins." So he said to the man, "I tell you, get up, take your mat and go home." He got up, took his mat and walked out in full view of them all. This amazed everyone and they praised God, saying, "We have never seen anything like this!"

THE AUDIBLE AND "STILL SMALL" VOICE OF GOD

A voice came from the cloud, saying, "This is my Son, whom I have chosen; listen to him."

—LUKE 9:35

Because of the verse above, the external, audible voice of God is the way most believers expect to hear from God. Many times in the Bible, God's voice seems to be outward in dramatic encounters. Much more frequently, however, the majority of people hear the still small voice that Elijah heard in 1 Kings 19:11-13. This still small voice is like a whisper in your ear but inside your head.

For Isaiah, however, the experience was an outer voice:

"Whether you turn to the right or to the left, your ears will hear a voice behind you, saying, 'This is the way; walk in it'"

—ISAIAH 30:21

Can you imagine being Isaiah? God tells him *ahead of time* that he will hear a voice behind him. I don't know about you, but I'd be looking over my shoulder all the time, waiting to hear the wondrous voice of God!

MEMORIES

One of the most fascinating ways that God speaks is through our memories. Our partnership with God is demonstrated through the recollection of what He has done. His active voice is present in our memory. John 14:26 is a great illustration of this: "But the Advocate, the Holy Spirit, whom the Father will send in my name, will teach you all things and will remind you of everything I have said to you."

In order to bring to remembrance what God has said, He actively speaks to us through our memories. We are hardwired to hear Him. Our brain is trained to remember natural things, but spiritual—or supernatural—memory comes out of His active voice.

Having eyes, do you not see? And having ears, do you not hear? And do you not remember ...?

—MARK 8:18, *NASB*

But the Helper, the Holy Spirit, whom the Father will send in My name, He will teach you all things, and bring to your remembrance all that I said to you.

—JOHN 14:26, *NASB*

I shall remember the deeds of the Lord; Surely I will remember Your wonders of old. I will meditate on all Your work and muse on Your deeds.

—PSALM 77:11, *NKJV*

FLASHBACKS

A flashback is the instantaneous knowledge of God's past involvement in a person's life, place, or thing. In Genesis 28:13, God provides Jacob with a flashback to when He had made a promise to his father, Isaac.

Sometimes when a flashback happens, a person is filled with a situational awareness of being somewhere before it happens. The natural world calls this déjà vu. But in God's *supernatural* realm, it is a prophetic flashback. The person experiencing the flashback is brought to the emotional, physical, mental, and spiritual awareness of a past event that never took place.

> There above it stood the LORD, and he said: "I am the LORD, the God of your father Abraham and the God of Isaac. I will give you and your descendants the land on which you are lying."
>
> —GENESIS 28:13

> I have heard all about you, LORD. I am filled with awe by your amazing works. In this time of our deep need, help us again as you did in years gone by. And in your anger, remember your mercy.
>
> —HABAKKUK 3:2, *NLT*

DIVINE REVELATIONS

God has set aside divine revelations of His word and His heart for those who are near to Him. His word is for everyone, but the mysteries of His word are only made available to those who value His heart. Divine revelation is present in the midst of the day and when connecting to God's written and spoken word:

"Then he opened their minds so they could understand the Scriptures"

—LUKE 24:45

VISITATIONS

God can visit us in any form He chooses. Balaam's donkey is a great case in point: when this stubborn prophet refused to listen to God, the Lord spoke through the mouth of his donkey to get his attention (see Numbers 22:21-39).

In Revelation 1:12, John was visited by God in visions, revelation, in a vivid encounter. Visitations are prevalent for those who are catalysts of faith, like the apostle John. Conversely, visitations in the Bible also happen to those in radical opposition of God. The apostle Paul is the perfect example, as he went from being a radical Pharisee who persecuted followers of Jesus to being one of the greatest Christians of all time.

Then I turned to see the voice that was speaking with me. And having turned I saw seven golden lampstands; and in the middle of the lampstands I saw one like a son of man, clothed in a robe reaching to the feet, and girded across His chest with a golden sash. His head and His hair were white like white wool, like snow; and His eyes were like a flame of fire. His feet were like burnished bronze, when it has been made to glow in a furnace, and His voice was like the sound of many waters. In His right hand He held seven stars, and out of His mouth came a sharp two-edged sword; and His face was like the sun shining in its strength.

When I saw Him, I fell at His feet like a dead man. And He placed His right hand on me, saying, "Do not be afraid; I am the first and the last, and the living One; and I was dead, and behold, I am alive forevermore, and I have the keys of death and of Hades."

—REVELATION 1:12-17, *NASB*

SCENTS AND SMELLS

We are naturally hardwired to smell. God created our ability to smell and knows how pleasing or disturbing it can be. He most definitely uses scents to speak to us. Both good and bad smells can indicate many things. Generally, God will build a history of smell with you and train your senses to discern them. It is not surprising that other religions worship with the sense of smell.

All your robes are fragrant with myrrh and aloes and cassia; from palaces adorned with ivory the music of the strings makes you glad.

—PSALM 45:8

But thanks be to God, who always leads us as captives in Christ's triumphal procession and uses us to spread the aroma of the knowledge of him everywhere.

—2 CORINTHIANS 2:14

DIVINE TRANSLATION/TRANSPORTATION

Translation is God communicating by the moving of your spirit. Transportation is God communicating by the moving of your body.

Though transportation is rare, there are several examples in the Bible. After the apostle Philip baptizes the Ethiopian eunuch, God transports him to the town of Azotus, a distance of 25-30 miles (see Acts 8:39-40).

Jesus was transported several times in Scripture after His resurrection (see Luke 24:13-43; Matthew 28:8-10).

Translation is when God moves you in the Spirit, such as when Gehazi was divinely translated in 2 Kings 5:26.

In contrast, God transported Enoch and moved him in body to another place (see Genesis 5:24; Hebrews 11:5).

> *Remember Him before the silver cord is broken and the golden bowl is crushed, the pitcher by the well is shattered and the wheel at the cistern is crushed; then the dust will return to the earth as it was, and the spirit will return to God who gave it.*
>
> —ECCLESIASTES 12:6-7, *NASB*

THOUGHTS

The Bible tells us that we can share the same headspace with God. First Corinthians 2:16 tells us, "'Who has known the mind of the Lord so as to instruct him?' But we have the mind of Christ." As we abide in Christ, spending time listening for the Shepherd's voice, we begin to realign our thoughts and develop a renewed mind (see Ephesians 4:23).

God desires to speak in the most basic ways in which you were created. In other words, He made our minds to align with His will; He wants to speak to us through our thoughts. Put another way, our thoughts are not just thoughts but points of access into the mind and heart of God.

Our memory is for past and present context. Our thoughts are for present and future context. Our natural process of thought is the gateway for God's thoughts.

> Do not conform to the pattern of this world, but be transformed by the renewing of your mind. Then you will be able to test and approve what God's will is—his good, pleasing and perfect will.
>
> —ROMANS 12:2

> For the Spirit God gave us does not make us timid, but gives us power, love and a sound mind.
>
> —2 TIMOTHY 1:7

> Call to me and I will answer you and tell you great and unsearchable things you do not know.
>
> —JEREMIAH 33:3

> Set your minds on things above, not on earthly things. For you died, and your life is now hidden with Christ in God. When Christ, who is your life, appears, then you also will appear with him in glory.
>
> —COLOSSIANS 3:2-4

7 | GIFTS OF THE HOLY SPIRIT

I love that God was thoughtful enough to design tools that would enable us to work with His Spirit and to really know how to partner with Him. With the Spirit deployed through Christ, God gave gifts and ministries to implement those gifts and steward His kingdom.

He is the God of yesterday, today and forever. No one can stop Him from giving His kids gifts—not denominations, movements, theological positions, or belief systems.

For by the grace given me I say to every one of you: Do not think of yourself more highly than you ought, but rather think of yourself with sober judgment, in accordance with the faith God has distributed to each of you. For just as each of us has one body with many members, and these members do not all have the same function, so in Christ we, though

*many, form one body, and each member be-
longs to all the others. We have different gifts,
according to the grace given to each of us.
If your gift is prophesying, then prophesy in
accordance with your faith; if it is serving,
then serve; if it is teaching, then teach; if it is
to encourage, then give encouragement; if it
is giving, then give generously; if it is to lead,
do it diligently; if it is to show mercy, do it
cheerfully.*

—ROMANS 12:3-8

Everyone has been given gifts!

According to this scripture, God bestowed grace upon us so that we can operate in our gifts. We have all been equipped with a special grace to contribute and to bring forth the reward of Jesus on the earth. Part of our purpose is to realize the grace that God has given to us, alongside the grace within these gifts, and to bring about His kingdom in our lives and the lives of those around us.

God saw fit to bestow upon us the nature of the Holy Spirit to partner with us in His work and as co-laborers in this kingdom. You see, these gifts were not created for a momentary expression. These gifts are part of God; He has elected to share them with us according to the terms of the New Covenant. Just as we partake of the death, burial, and resurrection of Christ, so too we should partake in the reward of Christ.

What follows is a comprehensive list of the biblical spiritual gifts (minus the fivefold ministry, which we covered previously).

1. Prophecy
2. Pastor
3. Teaching
4. Wisdom
5. Knowledge
6. Exhortation
7. Discerning of Spirits
8. Giving
9. Helps
10. Mercy
11. Missionary
12. Evangelist
13. Hospitality
14. Faith
15. Leadership
16. Administration
17. Miracles
18. Healing
19. Tongues
20. Interpretation
21. Intercession
22. Service

Much can be said about each gift that God provides. For the sake of this book, we will stick to prophecy. Nevertheless, one should know that God provides every person with gifts. Based on reason of use, God's grace can create a path of ministry within these gifts.

Think of God's gifts more like a partnership than a lottery. If you are actively desiring to partner with God and bring about His will on the earth, then how could He say no? He actually wants it more than you do, but He knows perfect timing, preparation, and circumstance better than anyone.

Our layered theology and denominational biases have prevented us from experiencing the simplicity of God. If you confess that Jesus is Lord, then it is only by the Holy Spirit that it is physically possible.

Furthermore, your confession, or salvation, is of the same means as the gifts of God. They are instantly available. Amazing! That is why in 1 Corinthians 1:12, the apostle Paul says, "I don't want anyone to be unaware."

Let's dive deeper into this amazing chapter of scripture:

> Now there are varieties of gifts, but the same Spirit. And there are varieties of ministries, and the same Lord. There are varieties of effects, but the same God who works all things in all persons. But to each one is given the manifestation of the Spirit for the common good. For to one is given the word of wisdom through the Spirit, and to another the word of knowledge according to the same Spirit; to another faith by the same Spirit, and to another gifts of healing by the one Spirit, and to another the effecting of miracles, and to another prophecy, and to another the distinguishing of spirits, to another various kinds of tongues, and to another the interpretation of tongues.
>
> —1 CORINTHIANS 12:4-10, *NASB*

It is by the same Spirit that we receive these bestowed active gifts. The Holy Spirit provides us with a dimension of grace that allows us to walk in supernatural gifting. The gifts are from the kingdom and accessible through the kingdom.

As Jesus clearly puts it, the kingdom of heaven is at hand. The kingdom of heaven is like a throttle: you can speed it up or you can slow it down. It's up to you. God's gifts are the same way. You can grow them or slow them down in your own life. With your active partnership, by exercising your senses, and through faithful practice, these gifts can grow in your life.

Many in the Bible walked in multiple gift sets. King David, for example, was a worshiper, apostle, and prophet. John the Baptist was an evangelist and prophet. The gifts go together more commonly than not. For example, prophecy often links with words of knowledge; words of knowledge with words of wisdom; prophecy with words of wisdom; words of knowledge with administration; faith with prophecy. They go together.

GIFT OF PROPHECY

Having then gifts differing according to the grace that is given to us, let us use them: if prophecy, let us prophesy in proportion to our faith; or ministry, let us use it in our ministering; he who teaches, in teaching.

—ROMANS 12:6-7, *NKJV*

Prophecy is woven into the indented design of Christ's body, His church. Without it we are void of the implementation of God's perfect design. Who is qualified? Everyone is qualified!

Just as a body, though one, has many parts, but all its many parts form one body, so it is with Christ. For we were all baptized by one Spirit so as to form one body...

—1 CORINTHIANS 12:12-13

Each one is given the manifestation of the Spirit for the common good (see 1 Corinthians 12:7). Everyone has been given gifts. Not even children are restricted from receiving the Spirit of God, as when God told Jeremiah, "The Lord said to me, 'Do not say, "I am too young"'" (see

Jeremiah 1:5-10). God's sufficient grace provides us with these gifts (see Romans 12:6).

Prophecy, which consists of comprehensible speech inspired by the Spirit, contributed to the mutual edification and encouragement of all present (see 1 Corinthians 14:20-25,39).

With prophecy, your affections lie in the fact that God knows you and has plans for you. Knowing God's plans and future for your life gives you the opportunity to partner with Him to actually see those plans fulfilled.

It is my belief that everyone is given the ability to prophesy at the base level of the gift, or else Paul wouldn't have told us to pursue it in 1 Corinthians 14:1. Other evidence of God's desire for all His children to prophesy is Acts 2, where it says "all" the people gathered were filled with the Holy Spirit and prophesied in different languages.

Have you ever given someone an encouraging thought or strengthening message? That is the entrance to prophecy. In that instance, for a moment, you may have searched in your heart and mind for where the person could be (emotionally, physically, mentally, spiritually).

You had an inkling, a foretelling of them being somewhere better than right now, even a small upgrade, and you spoke that into existence. That is the start of prophecy—something that is inspirational. Inspirational words are the first step in the gift of prophecy.

The apostle Paul encourages us not to turn away from prophecy. In 1 Thessalonians 5:20, Paul pleads with us not to despise prophetic utterances.

God will entrust His gifts to us based on His will and on our ability to have proper stewardship over the gift. We already know God's will is to speak to us; we have established that.

Do we have the desire and discipline to apply stewardship?

We start with "all may prophesy" (1 Corinthians 14:31). Then we progress to those who are pursuing prophecy and grow and learn more with each use. Further along, God creates a means for the gift that we exercise in our lives as a ministry. Then, some will be seated in the office of prophet, and God will entrust to them an area of influence to govern, teach, and build the Church.

The gift of prophecy is progressive—if you so desire it to be in your life. Prophecy provides us access to all mysteries and all knowledge in Him. And because of this, God invites those who faithfully pursue intimacy and relationship with Him to have the grace for this gift.

WORDS OF KNOWLEDGE

The Bible is full of words-of-knowledge stories. In the Old Testament, we see prophets, leaders, and judges exercising this gift. In the New Testament, there are a variety of examples, starting with Elizabeth, who immediately knew Mary was pregnant.

I love how Elizabeth's word of knowledge came because of her own baby (John the Baptist) kicking within her. God gave her the honor of receiving a word of knowledge that Mary was pregnant with the Messiah (see Luke 1:41-44). Only God could have revealed that to her!

Ananias had a word of knowledge about Saul and went to commission him. He knew exactly where to find him—even down to the street name and address.

A few other examples:

- Elisha receives a clear picture of Naman's lie (see 2 Kings 5).

- Jesus sees Nathaniel under the fig tree (see John 1:47-50).

- Jesus knows what the disciples were arguing about (see Mark 9:33-35).

The apostles had various stories of words of knowledge, and when we study early Christianity it seems that this was a respected gift even after biblical times. Not only is there ample biblical precedence for words of knowledge, but this type of prophetic ministry happened a lot, and for many different reasons! God loves to share His thoughts and intentions with us about current and past events.

In Scripture, God uses words of knowledge to point out where to find people; to give provision; to provide details about who people were, including details about their life and health; to give direction on whom to appoint into leadership; to reveal who was going to die; to tell who was in the womb; and many other examples.

Throughout the Bible, God consistently gives divine knowledge to man so that we can fully relate to His goodness and eternal glory. He uses words of knowledge to show that He is very present and very connected to us. He created this awesome gift to illuminate what is in His heart and what He is thinking.

Throughout Scripture God could have chosen many ways to get the job done, but often He relied on flesh-and-blood people to deliver divine knowledge, which then served as a catalyst for His will and plans.

My book *God Secrets: A Life Filled with Words of Knowledge* is a one-of-a-kind book written on this amazing gift. I invite you to go deeper on the subject.

WORDS OF WISDOM

A word of wisdom is God-inspired application for a given person, place, thing, or situation. It brings divine instruction: how to and how God would. Contextually speaking, a word of wisdom is what Jesus would do in any given situation. Commonly used alongside the other revelatory gifts, words of wisdom are actual wisdom that God gives us.

Such prophetic words help us know how to apply our plans, and even other prophetic words, to our lives. When it is a word, wisdom is like instruction. Think of it as heaven coaching you on how to plan and pursue who you are or what you're called to, or how to love those who are part of your destiny.

When God imparted His knowledge and wisdom to King Solomon, people came from every nation just to hear him deliver justice and rule his kingdom in his courts. It was so awesome that it became a spectacle. This supernatural knowledge affected the way his kingdom was built and how justice was applied on a political and judicial scale.

Solomon's words of wisdom impacted not only Israel but also every known nation on Earth. The king asked for the prophetic gifts of words and wisdom and knowledge, and we can see them being downloaded into his very nature in 1 Kings 3:9: "So give your servant a discerning heart to govern your people and to distinguish between right and wrong. For who is able to govern this great people of yours?"

The word "understanding" that Solomon asks for is the Hebrew word *shama,* which means to hear intelligently. It directly reflects his desire to have God's intelligence on what he hears. The word "discern" in Hebrew is *biyn,* which means to distinguish, be cunning, have intelligence or knowledge between, to understand.

Solomon's request involving both *shama* and *biyn* is the first time in the Bible that a person asks to think like God thinks. Solomon was literally asking to have the mind of God, to receive knowledge and wisdom like God.

Similarly, in the life of Daniel and his friends, we see a picture of revelation downloaded for the sake of education. Daniel says, "As for these four youths God gave them knowledge and skill in all learning and wisdom and Daniel understanding in all kinds of visions and dreams" (Daniel 1:17, *AMP*).

The word "knowledge" used here is the Hebrew word *madda.* This is both the word for divine intelligence and also divine consciousness. This is a perfect description for words of knowledge where you have a divine consciousness of what is in God's mind and intelligence.

Both the gift of knowledge and wisdom combined to take Daniel and his comrades beyond a natural education, and affected how their leadership impacted Babylon.

God longs to share the best of Himself with a people who would be worthy of it, and words of knowledge are one of the assimilators of His nature.

DISCERNMENT

But solid food is for the mature, who because of practice have their senses trained to discern good and evil.

—HEBREWS 5:14

For followers of Christ, discernment is the God-inspired identification of an unseen spiritual reality. We receive it by having God's Spirit living inside of us, responding to the world around us. As we pursue discernment, God helps us to perceive the variables of good versus evil in any given person, place, thing or situation.

We can apply discernment to every area of life. All of heaven can be discerned, as well as the things of Earth.

We also have natural discernment (as opposed to *super*natural); another word for this is common intuition. God created us with the ability to intuit (perceive, sense, have an inkling about) each other's motives, hearts, gifts, talents, and skills.

Prophecy and natural or spiritual discernment are completely different things. Whereas a person can have discernment without being prophetic, a person who is prophetic always employs discernment. In other words, all humanity is hardwired for discernment; it is part of the way God made us, even before we give our lives to Christ.

Discernment—whether the gift or the intuitive type—is only a conversation starter with God and is not the prophetic. It helps people, but we have to get His perceptions about our discernment or we often times get in trouble or violate love. I teach about this extensively in other books and materials.

As we enter into a life in Christ, God flips the switch on the power source of the Holy Spirit. Now our natural ability to perceive becomes a supernatural ability to discern. As we exercise God-driven discernment through intimacy with Christ (e.g., prayer times, worship, flexing our spiritual gifts and growing in them), our ability to discern, feel, or sense the things God wants us to sense heightens and increases. It's a relational tool, but it is not a substitute for relationship itself.

When you discern things, you're not necessarily getting a prophetic message of revelation. It's God's Spirit in you causing a reaction in your spirit. This is more of a conversation starter. It's God helping your spirit man use your spiritual eyes and feelings to know and glimpse the world around you.

Discernment involves all the senses plus your spiritual senses working together, and they are God's gifts of connection to you. Connect with God first and allow your discernment to be the door for spiritual revelation that goes beyond your thoughts, feelings, opinions, or faith. God wants you to take what you discern and talk to Him about it. Then He can reveal His deep heart and share His thoughts about it.

DISCERNMENT VS. PROPHECY

A lot of words given by a "prophet" are just words of discernment, and nothing more. In such cases, the giver of the word has not gone beyond his own mind and heart and traveled into God's. That takes connection. Anyone can discern something if he listens for a moment, but only Christians can consistently pursue the heart of God through His Spirit and hear what He is saying about their discernment.

Christianity has had some of the greatest moves of God come directly out of California, but also some of the worst moral indiscretions—from Christian leaders to Christian cults to imbalanced Christian-focused media. Southern California was the Wild West of the Church for a while. Discerning what is wrong with California is easy. Discerning what is right is a little harder, but not that difficult.

Discerning God's heart for what He wants for California only comes by revelation and intimacy. Many people have assumed that because so many revivals have come out of California, we are assured of a revival from here again. Conversely, other people assume, in their faith-based perspective, that because so much evil has come out of California, Californians are doomed in the long term.

Both of these assumptions can be birthed out of deep presumption. I know what God wants because I have read about Him; I have heard what He has done before and will do again. I have deep knowledge of His principles; I have seen Him act throughout biblical history.

Our goal is to grow in our ability to perceive the mind and heart of Christ, including thoughts and intentions. We don't assume to know the answer based on spiritual information, discernment, or experience. We go deeper and "hear" what He is thinking.

John 3:17 says that Jesus didn't come into the world to convict us of sin—that's the Holy Spirit's job. For us, we are to emulate Jesus: love the world, show people who they are, and help them to see the safe boundaries around the revelation of Christ's love.

When people see who God is and what He wants, and if they want to be connected to God, they will protect that connection at all costs once they experience it. If we only give the principles of God's kingdom, however, and fail to give a revelation of God's character, then people will never come—or *want* to come—into a place of relationship with Him. Who wants to worship a rules-only, grace-less God?

To activate discernment for kingdom advancement, we need to:

- Actively listen for God's voice and not just pull from past experiences
- Use the Word of God as our filter, not current events
- Try not to always default to what we know or have known (hearing His voice is a big experiment)
- Push beyond negativity (our own, any known facts about who we are speaking to)
- Understand that prophecy is not based upon the things we have failed in

THE OFFICE OF PROPHET

And God hath set some in the church, first apostles, secondarily prophets, thirdly teachers, after that miracles, then gifts of healings, helps, governments, diversities of tongues.

—1 CORINTHIANS 12:28, *KJV*

I want to look at the differences between prophets in the Old Testament and those in the New Testament. And there are several differences that are a game changer when it comes to how we pursue these gifts.

We have already established that the fivefold government is a gift from Jesus to the Church. Viewing the office of prophet in this light will really help us to celebrate what it can become. It is actually the most spoken-about office in the entire Bible.

As a refresher, there is a difference between someone who prophesies and someone who is seated in the office of a prophet. All believers are encouraged to prophesy (see 1 Corinthians 14); not all are called into the fivefold gift of prophet.

More than 100 prophets are called by name in the Bible. Also, there are more than 1,000 prophets mentioned in the Bible, but not by name. This forms a very different picture when you see it from this angle.

Imagine with me for a moment the days of Obadiah, a prophet who rescued 100 prophets because of the actions of Ahab (see 1 Kings 18:4). I am amazed that God gathered 100 prophets in one place. When was the last time you were in a room of 100 God-confirmed prophets? That is some powerful imagery.

The strength of the office was tremendous and revered among everyone in those days—and there were 100 of them! What could you do in your country, industry, or government with 100 prophets present?

I remember a time when I was part of leadership for a group of more than 250 prophetic people in community and attending a church in Kansas City. For a season of time, we would meet once a month to receive instruction and to garner feedback from the previous month's gathering. At the end, we would give and receive prophetic revelation.

About a year into our group gatherings, there was a month when more than thirty people had the same dream! As you can imagine, this amazing prophetic "flash mob" was extremely encouraging to the leadership of the church. There were also times when five to eight people would receive the same prophetic warning through very similar experiences.

My favorite experience, however, was when a directive message would come to twenty or more people. As leaders, we were so excited to witness how God was crafting our community by His voice and taking such wonderful care of us.

It was beautiful!

OCCUPATIONAL THEMES OF PROPHETS

We see in Scripture some themes for the purpose of prophets and their occupation:

1. The prophet is called to prepare humanity for what God is about ready to do (see Luke 27).

2. In this, they lay the foundation of the Church (see Ephesians 2:20).

3. The office lends itself to the whole body of Christ, fostering holiness and direction for regions, cities, and nations, establishing kingdom values and experiences that build up the Church.

4. They build one person and organization at a

time with the Spirit of prophecy using the secrets of God (see Amos 3:7).

5. They operate in the authority of God's will. They don't conduct their own agenda; they operate in the name of the Lord. The name of the Lord is a Hebrew idiom that means "in the authority of the Lord" and "in the character of the Lord." They operate in His authority, which brings accompanying fruit and signs to their life.

6. Holistically, the prophet is a governing mediatory for God's people. In modern times this would be viewed as a responsibility along with apostles and other fivefold leaders to help govern the Church.

     Moses was a powerful prophet of God who actively petitioned the heart and mind of God as a mediator for the Church (see Exodus 32:7-14,30-35; Numbers 14:13-19). It is my belief that Moses knew what God ultimately wanted and pursued a process to bring about His will.

7. The prophets in the Old Testament were essentially a proxy for the Holy Spirit to the people. They partnered with God to bring forth His will to the people to comfort them, provide miracles, procure supernatural food (e.g., manna from heaven), bring direction and protection, and provide an atonement process to lead people to Jesus, among many other things. People petitioned prophets as their mediatory

between them and God. Their prophecies carried revelation, activation, impartation, direction, and confirmation.

In stark contrast, in the New Testament, we are all given access to the will of God and connection to God through the Holy Spirit. Jesus restored our connection with God! We no longer need a proxy through which we commune with our loving Creator. Jesus built a bridge that crosses the chasm of our sin to connect us directly with the Father's love.

We are each justified by our own faith and have no need of a mediator. We now have Jesus and His Spirit of truth, revelation, wisdom, and knowledge living inside of us.

CATEGORIES OF PROPHETS

Let's now review categories for the office of prophet in the Old and New Testaments. We study these contrasts because it is through such evaluation of past prophets' words, actions, and lives that we find context, meaning, understanding, and application.

In chapter 2, we examined the historical context for prophecy and established the need for the office of prophet. This need was driven by God's desire to speak to His people and lead them in the right direction. Let's review the five types discussed previously, and then look at these five categories in our modern context for prophets.

1. Messianic prophecies—all prophecies relating to Jesus

2. Law-establishing and abiding prophecies—all

prophecies relating to the creation and adherence of the Law

3. Purpose and potential prophecies—all prophecies related to one's purpose, destiny, dreams, and capabilities; to strengthening, encouraging, and comforting

4. Building the body of Christ prophecies—corporate unification, edification of the Church, God's will in a city, governance, etc.

5. Future-preparedness prophecies—warnings, plans, and direction

In order to establish an acceptable context for the office of prophet today, we need to create some distinctions from past prophecies, roles of prophets, and applications. The context for prophecy and prophets has changed a lot from the Old Testament until now. We know and accept that all Scripture is sufficient for every good work, so we will value it and apply it to our lives with proper context (see 2 Timothy 3:17).

1. Messianic Prophecies

In the New Testament, after Jesus fulfilled His purpose, no one needs to prophesy the historical coming of Jesus, what He will bring to us, and what He will do for us (i.e., messianic prophecies). In the Old Testament, however, we needed messianic prophecies to establish the historical context for Jesus.

Nevertheless, He has already come. He has already conquered the grave. He is our present-day King. According to the New Testament, Jesus is the present-day ruler over the kings of the earth (see Revelation 1:5).

2. LAW-ESTABLISHING AND LAW-ABIDING PROPHECIES

In the Old Testament, God's people did not desire a prophetic relationship with Him. So, God established a standard of truth through the giving and adherence of the Law. Well, Jesus brought about a perfect fulfillment to the Law and the old season of prophets (see Matthew 11:13). He did not destroy the Law, because by itself it was right, just, and perfect in the eyes of God.

It was only when the perfect Law was placed next to sin that it looked bad. God brought a fulfillment to the Law; Christ was the fulfillment. All who choose to accept Jesus Christ receive freedom from the Law. If someone chooses not to accept Jesus, they still live under the Law. For it is by the Law that we see the context for freedom and how it is made possible in Jesus. Thus, Jesus is the only way to receive a fulfillment of the Law.

If the Law is fulfilled in Christ, then there is no reason for us to prophesy its statutes outside of the context of Jesus. The entire Old Testament needs to be realized and actualized in the Person of Christ. Jesus brought about a solution to the identified problem within the Law that the Old Testament prophets were trying to solve. The problem, of course, was that no matter what sacrifices were made, or what statutes were observed, God's people continually fell short of the mark (i.e., the payment of sin is death).

The answer is that we need to reconfigure our thoughts to be in agreement with Jesus. In other words, we don't live under the Law anymore. And so, New Testament prophets are only permitted to prophesy out of the Law if they are establishing their fulfillment in Christ Jesus or the finished work that He accomplished.

Much of the will of God is made available through the Law and defined further in Christ Jesus. Humanity is not in need of any Law-establishing prophecies anymore. The Law has already been established. What humanity will continue to need, though, is to hear God's will through both His Word and through prophecy. We will always need to have prophetic understanding and application of the will of God in our natural, spiritual, and emotional lives.

(We will assess the reward of Jesus and the will of the Father in a later section of the book.)

3. Purpose and Potential Prophecies

Purpose and potential prophecies have only just begun. We have found the most beautiful representation of the Father in Christ Jesus, and in Him, people's hearts were made bare and their dreams were made possible. A perfect example of this is the woman at the well who had been married five times and was living with a man who was not her husband.

After Jesus spoke to her, she professed that Jesus told her everything there ever was to know about her. She felt completely known, heard, loved, accepted. And out of this place, she brought ministry and transformation to her entire village (see John 4:1-42).

Prophets in the Old and New Testaments called forth people into their ultimate calling, interpreted their dreams, and spoke their callings into existence. God has a vested interest in us. The continuation of this type of prophecy is more than just desired; it's essential for the whole of humanity so that we can become the best version of ourselves.

4. BUILDING THE BODY OF CHRIST PROPHECIES

More than ever before, the body of Christ needs to be built up in the way that we should go. Old and New Testament prophets have always called for the unification and edification of the Church. God desires to continue to establish the governing prophecies of building up His Church. I should mention, God's Church is not a building or a temple.

The apostle Paul gives us language for this when he asks, "Did you not know that you are the temple of God?" (see 1 Corinthians 3:16). The building up of the body of Christ is the corporate building, edification, and unification of the body of Jesus.

5. FUTURE-PREPAREDNESS PROPHECIES

The context for God leading and guiding His people will never go away. And although future-preparedness prophecies were only a small part of the prophets' contribution throughout both Testaments, they will indeed continue for wonderful reasons. The availability of this type of prophecy is contingent upon the availability of God's voice.

There is much to learn about future-preparedness prophecies. There are many pitfalls to avoid when discussing this type of prophecy. In the past, a lot of people have mistaken their discernment or fear for prophecy when it comes to future warnings, judgment, and direction. As California residents, we kind of chuckle when someone prophesies that there will be a great earthquake here.

That is like predicting that a hurricane will hit Florida, or that a tornado is going to sweep through Oklahoma.

We will be discussing the pitfalls of future-preparedness prophecies in later chapters.

Through Christ, we find perfect fulfillments of the Law, and we also see tremendous potential in this New Covenant.

Now let's look at what the qualifiers are for Old and New Testament prophets. We will need to keep in mind the context of these words and our present-day access to solutions in Christ.

This is going to be exciting!

8 | QUALIFIERS FOR A PROPHET

I wanted to lay out the importance of prophets in the Bible and what a New Covenant prophet looks like, as well as the qualifiers for recognizing one. This doesn't limit the gift or ministry available to every single Christian, but it can help to celebrate and recognize when God does choose to appoint someone to the office of prophet.

As we established before, the offices are from Jesus and will bear great fruit. These are not roles you can choose for yourself, and you cannot make yourself a prophet. Have you ever been to a conference where someone hands you a business card that reads, "John Doe, Electrical Engineer/Prophet"? I have!

The gift of being a prophet is not self-proclaimed. It is helpful to understand that the office of prophet is a divinely appointed role. The prophet then must be recognized by an established *ekklesia* (or church), denomination, or organization for the building up of God's people.

Many people who claim to be a prophet probably don't have a full understanding of what it means to be one. As a matter of fact, most who use the title "prophet" are probably just people pursuing the prophetic gifts, which is great. They might even be excelling at giving prophetic words. However, simply because a person prophesies and is pursuing the prophetic does not make them a prophet.

This is not to dissuade or discourage you if you believe God is calling you into a deeper understanding and practice of the prophetic. Indeed, it is a process, and learning to prophesy will take some down the road to this appointment.

There are qualifiers that we can look at to see if a person is actually on the journey of becoming a prophet. These can also be measured by the fruit of their actual life as well.

A man from a very small town in the South here in America emailed me a long prophetic word. It warned of judgments that were about to come to my city in the form of a natural disaster that would rival Hurricane Katrina. (You may recall that Katrina decimated vast parts of the Gulf Coast of the U.S. in 2005, including the city of New Orleans.)

I had never heard from this man before, but he (or members of his team) kept referring to "The Prophet," and I realized it was either him in the third person or someone writing for him. It was awkward—and the word was even worse. I emailed back and asked him what ministry or church he was a part of.

I received the following reply: "I am under God's covering!"

This is a typical excuse for people who are not under the biblical authority of a church or movement, or who have no authentication for the role they are trying to play. I then asked him to send me some other prophetic words that had proven accurate in how they had played out (his prophetic history). Simply put, I wanted to see some history and references.

He had none, but he had a really funny answer: "Thus sayith the Lord of hosths you are to listen to me!"

He spelled two words wrong in that statement, and I realized a few things. As I read that, I wondered if *he* was now the Lord because he was demanding that I listen to him. Or even worse, if the Lord my God had forgotten how to spell.

I have no problem listening to the Lord, but if this uneducated "prophet" thought I was going to listen to him, then he had a very delusional sense of theology and life. He was obviously a false prophet, which was easy to see.

Please know that God loves a false prophet just as much as a real one. I realize this man was most likely dealing with some deep wounds or unresolved issues, or perhaps even mental illness. My point is not to condemn him but to clarify that not everyone who claims to hear from God actually does!

Another tip-off is if I receive a long email in ALL CAPITAL LETTERS. For some reason, false prophets love the caps lock key on their keyboard! Usually, false prophets display such bad behavior that they are easy to recognize. They often display a lack of love and care for the world around them. And usually there is a judgmental, condemning spirit or tone that accompanies their prophecies.

All joking aside, it can be hard to recognize the signs of a person who is a candidate for the office of prophet. It can be difficult to know how to appoint prophets and check for the fruit of their ministry. The process, however, is very much worth the effort—we need to get the most out of this incredible office, which is such a powerful tool for Christianity. (We will go into greater detail on identifying false prophets in chapter 9.)

The scriptural qualifiers and examples for appointing prophets are laid out and clear to see when looked for. We can come into an empowered position of receiving not only prophetic words but also prophets.

Many people are called prophet today, especially in some Pentecostal and charismatic circles. This makes it hard to know when this is a true appointment or when it's simply a church's style to use names as titles of respect. In other words, is "Prophet Bill" actually a prophet with biblical authority or simply a well-respected leader in the church?

We don't need to appoint people into titles—that is God's job, and He guides us along the way. Many churches and movements, however, use titles to help establish people's expectations of these roles. This can be helpful in some circles, but it can also lead to inaccurate labeling where people get false identity built through it, which can lead to segregation.

True prophets don't need the title or recognition to be seen as a prophet. They are known by what God accomplishes through their relationship with the Holy Spirit and the revelation that is brought to the world around them. They don't even need to tell their own stories to build others' faith; prophets usually have so many remarkable stories that others spread them around before the prophet even shows up!

I have met many people with the name "prophet" who didn't bear the fruit of a prophet. Titles without fruit are equal to Jesus walking up to the fig tree, excited to eat the fruit from a tree whose leaves were large and green. It turned out, however, that the tree bore no fruit at all (see Matthew 12:11-25). And what did Jesus do? He cursed the tree, and it remained forever barren.

Authentic prophets operate by the Spirit of God, not by their title. In saying that, I have no problem with establishing the prophetic office or title when it is done in connection with the administration of the office. The expectations need to be clearly set, the qualifiers put in place, and the relational connection made with the people to whom they are called to be a prophet.

As we evaluate people whom we think God is calling into the office of prophet, we need to set our beliefs and biases aside. We need to let God be the one who confirms their calling, and to search for the fruit that is born from their prophetic ministry. Simple "fruit checks," such as tracking their prophetic words, can help us see if we should receive them as a prophet.

Many people who are called prophets don't have a track record that can be measured. Even worse, they have shared prophetic words on the Internet or in public that have consistently been inaccurate or plain wrong—more than their prophecies that have been accurate. And of course, if they don't have accountability, it's impossible to know if they are called to be a prophet.

If what a prophet proclaims in the name of the Lord does not take place or come true, that is a message the Lord has not spoken.

—DEUTERONOMY 18:22

As I have said, one of my favorite modern prophets was Bob Jones. Driven by his intimate friendship with God,

Bob's prophecies and revelations helped more people and movements than anyone I know. Everyone who met Bob felt like he was a father, brother, or grandpa, including me—someone who never had a grandfather present. But I had Bob.

Bob always spoke with a scriptural understanding and often would quote passages of the Bible along with his prophetic words. This biblical prophetic bedrock gave everyone such a passion to connect to Scripture. He would give words that gave people faith and moved many personal dreams forward.

But Bob also gave blueprint or prototype words that established many ministries, including Morningstar Ministries, Bethel Church Ministry School in Redding, California, the International House of Prayer in Kansas City, the Call with Lou Engle, and the list goes on. He had a remarkable ability to activate other prophets and fivefold ministry people and was one of the most sought-after prophets of our generation.

His calendar was always full of people wanting to meet with him to receive impartation and prayer. And many people had "before and after" moments with Bob. In other words, his intimacy with the Father and his finely tuned prophetic gifting gave him the ability to bring clarity to each person's revelation, no matter how small. As a result, God used him mightily to put value on the usefulness of a person's experiences.

Bob prophesied in parables most of the time, so he needed community around him to help his words land in the full capacity of what they were meant to be. He often needed interpretation from others to help bring clarity to what he was saying, but he was so open and accountable.

Sometimes, though, he would give such specific words that it was frightening.

He would point on a map and tell people to drive 50 miles west and look for a certain sign, turn down that street and knock on a door of a certain house. These would be places he never visited, and the miracles from these types of encounters were crazy!

His track record included many very specific and incredible words that whole movements would include as part of their story or history when sharing their testimony. This track record also could be filtered to understand which types of words he gave had the most authority and even which types of words were less weighty.

I remember one of my own stories with Bob. One day he contacted me and told me that I would have a heavenly encounter that day. He then said that I should call him later that afternoon so that he could explain it to me. That got my attention!

That day was one of the busiest of my life, and I lost track of even trying to pray or be available for the encounter.

But it happened anyway.

It was so confusing because I saw a vision of two chains across Mickey Mouse's head and a blindfold across his eyes. I called Bob and told him, not expecting much. It didn't seem that profound because it just popped into my head. It might have just been me, but it was the only thing out of the ordinary that day.

Bob was elated. He told me that I was about to have an impact with God's desire over the Walt Disney Company and that I would have many divine appointments with Disney people. He said that the company was blind to its original purpose of why God created it; that is why Mickey had the blindfold on.

He said that the chains represented bureaucracy and unions (he was not against unions in general, but he said that the unions were blocking the family from coming forth). He prophesied that I would meet many Disney employees in my life and would help them to come into faith for their purpose in the company.

This vision and prophetic interpretation came right after my family and I had moved to L.A. and started our ministry. What was the first studio we were invited to come lead a prayer meeting in? Disney! Over the proceeding eleven years, I have met probably more than fifty Disney employees who have sought me out to hear from God about their life and occupation.

Many times, as I have prophesied to Disney employees, I have seen blindfolds falling off and chains being broken.

The key is that Bob took the time to hear from God on my behalf. He was obedient to give the word to me and to encourage me as a new resident of Los Angeles. That simple vision has helped me to understand how to pray for Disney employees, from top-level studio executives to the folks working at Disneyland.

Because of Bob's amazing vision, I have faith for God to move within the Disney Company, as I continue to receive invitations to pray, lead Bible studies, and spend time with executives of the different Disney divisions.

In this sense, I learned one of the most valuable lessons of what a modern prophet does for people with whom they relate: A modern prophet establishes faith for what God is already telling a person and can often interpret a prophetic word so that the individual will have a useful model for what God is saying.

Bob Jones was one of the ones that it was easy to see was qualified to be a prophet because he had the fruit in his life.

THE QUALIFIERS OF A PROPHET

Let's assess some of the qualifiers of being a prophet, and also the fruits. These are the essential features and elements that modern prophets possess:

THE ANOINTING—Modern prophets must have the anointing. Another way to say it is to have evidence of the Spirit of God upon them: "I wish that all the Lord's people were prophets and that the Lord would put his Spirit on them" (Numbers 11:29). This sounds like a huge, ominous qualifier, but it will become glaringly obvious if the person is operating out of God's supernatural spirit of revelation.

JESUS PLUS NOTHING—Prophets speak for Him. Jesus is their only connection to revelation, and it is through relationship with Him that they get this revelation. They don't have other spirits, saints, totems, guides, etc.—just God through the name of Jesus. This isn't just about saying His name; it is about fully representing Him and all of the revelation and heart behind it—which points to His kingship. We enter into partnership with heaven in giving Jesus His full reward.

ACCURATE PROPHECIES—A genuine prophet's messages come true the majority of the time. They are vindicated or authorized by the fulfillment of their message (see Jeremiah 14:14).

FULL OBEDIENCE—Prophets practice absolute obedience to what they are hearing: "But I can't say whatever

I please. I must speak only what God puts in my mouth" (Numbers 22:38).

INTEGRITY—A central virtue that qualifies a prophet is moral integrity. Honesty would be one of the central themes of this integrity. As a matter of fact, false prophets are often identified as liars; they are self-gratifying or doing it for their own fame. When you see a prophet with integrity, it is obvious.

GOD ANOINTED AND APPOINTED—Prophets are appointed by God. They are not chosen or elected by people, and they are not permitted to inherit the title from someone else. God appoints prophets. All the Church can do is recognize their divine calling and appoint it within their lives, movements, and churches. Deuteronomy 18:15 points out that "the Lord your God will raise up for you a prophet like me from among you, from your fellow Israelites." Notice that it says *from* the Israelites—not *by* them.

HUMILITY—Integrity's twin virtue is humility; you can't have one without the other. Humility is a byproduct of integrity. The prophets of the Old Testament were faithful, blameless and humble men (see Genesis 6:9). Unfortunately, humility can seem like a lost art in some facets of modern ministry. Some modern prophets operate out of their "expertise" and seem to be know-it-alls.

A true prophet actually is humble and realizes that they don't know everything. They are on an exploration journey and acknowledge the fact that they have not seen everything and don't have all the answers. One of the beautiful safety nets of the prophetic is when someone is dependent on God and doesn't have all the answers—even when sought out. When someone becomes the source of God's voice *for* you, instead of acting as an encourager to God's voice *in* you, this is often pride masking as ministry.

COMPASSION—Over and over in Scripture we see prophets moved by compassion to bring God's will to Earth. Think of Elisha with the mother whose son was dead (see 2 Kings 4:8-38), Samuel telling Saul his father's donkeys had been found and were okay (see 1 Samuel 9), etc.

COMMITTED TO SCRIPTURE—True prophets always prophesy in agreement with Scripture (see Exodus 34:27).

BOLDNESS—Prophets do whatever God tells them to do, even if it is not socially normal or "cool." Jeremiah 1:5-10 says, "Because everywhere I send you, you shall go, And all that I command you, you shall speak" (*NASB*). God's voice is central to everything that prophets do. They are never commissioned to act on their own, without His voice—neither in the Old Testament nor in the New Testament, nor today.

AUTHORITY—God gives them consistent authority. In His wisdom, He chooses men and women who obey Him faithfully and He gives them authority to speak on His behalf.

REFLECT GOD'S NATURE—They reveal the nature of God; they are not just giving prophetic words (see Deuteronomy 5:4-10).

LIVES LIKE PARABLES—Their lives, or specific seasons of their journey, are parabolic for the people they are called to minister. We see this over and over—God makes His people signs and symbols (see Isaiah 8:18).

A SOLID TRACK RECORD—They have a track record that is easily accessible so that others can clearly see whether their prophecies have come to pass. Linked to this is an identifiable amount of spiritual fruit flowing from the lives of those to whom they have given prophetic words. It's not just that the prophet can tell their own story; their story is being told. Modern prophets reflect the truth of Jeremiah 28:9: "But the prophet who prophesies peace will be recognized as one truly sent by the Lord only if his prediction comes true" (see also Ezekiel 33:33).

FRUITS OF THE OFFICE

Now that we know the biblical characteristics that qualify a person for the office of prophet, let's look at what the outgrowth is: the fruit.

GOD'S PRESENCE—God is present with prophets in obvious ways (see Exodus 3:1-12). Consider Paul Cain, a 1950s healing evangelist turned prophet. He had a season where the dignity of the prophetic office was so sought after that he even addressed Congress prophetically—publicly and on record. He was known for giving the Clinton administration prophetic words about not going to war with Iran. His assignment as a prophet was endorsed so strongly by both God and the U.S. government that he was sent to Iraq for "diplomatic purposes" to meet with Saddam Hussein. He gave Saddam such a confirming prophetic word that it just may have diverted a third major war with Iraq (after the Gulf War, and before 9/11).

God was so present with Paul Cain that even Saddam Hussein said, "I have many prophets like you, but they are not filled with God like you. They can predict things, but they don't know God." I wonder how much Saddam thought of Paul and his words from a Father who still loved him while hiding in a pit toward the end of his life?

Dignity—They dignify the prophetic to outsiders and people who don't necessarily believe God still speaks today:

> But the servant replied, "Look, in this town there is a man of God; he is highly respected, and everything he says comes true. Let's go there now. Perhaps he will tell us what way to take."
>
> —1 SAMUEL 9:6

I have personally seen this happen so many times. One of my favorite experiences, however, was when I was meeting with a group of designers from one of the most popular tech companies in the world. It seemed as if they were not believers, and I was having lunch with a friend who introduced me to them.

I took a risk while on their campus, and while I was standing over them as they were eating, God dropped a word in my spirit. I asked, "What does Scorpio mean?" One of them said, "How does he know the name of our project?" Another looked at our mutual friend to see if he had been talking but realized he didn't know the name of the confidential project. (The name isn't Scorpio—I changed it for confidentiality.)

The main team leader responded with his own question: "What does it mean to you?" I prophesied, "I am a Christian and I know this sounds weird, but I feel like you guys were about to lose funding in your department. This project, however, will be your saving grace and actually put your team on the map of the company in a fresh way. God loves you guys and has given you the gift of technology and wants to use you in a huge way."

They were all so confused and excited. It turns out that they were on the chopping block as a department but were working on something new that I couldn't explain to you even if I tried. My word of knowledge made God more real than probably anything else I could have said. Since then, my friend has followed up with the group, and most of them have come to the company Bible study to check it out. They all have a new belief in God and prophecy!

THE FEAR OF GOD—The fear of God follows the office of prophet (see Genesis 20:7). I was with a prophet named Cindy Jacobs who shared a word with a governmental leader. She shared two options for an approaching political choice. She could only have known his options by divine revelation, and the leader knew this. If he chose the corrupt path, she told him the effect it would have on his administration.

But she also shared that if he chose the harder option, and followed the Lord, beautiful opportunities would come, even for his family. He was gripped by the fear of God to hear so much confidential information from someone outside of his country. Cindy was sharing details that she otherwise could not know; it could have only been God's revelation. There was no way he was going down the road of corruption. The experience created a fear of God, or a protection of what God's will was for him. It caused him to see the black and white of his decision—there was no more grey area.

MIRACLES AND SIGNS—Godly prophets have miracles and signs to support their authority.

Several years ago, I was ministering with an incredible prophet named John Paul Jackson. We were in front of a group of people who didn't really believe in the prophetic power that had been embraced by our leader at the time, Mike Bickle.

Mike had just finished preaching and asked John Paul and me to come on stage to prophesy. John Paul pointed at one of the most unbelieving leaders in the room and said, "You had a dream last Friday night about your daughter. This is what happened in the dream and this is what God says about it."

It was very specific and I still remember inside my head screaming, *This is like walking out pages of the Bible! God is so awesome!* The man cried as he confirmed the dream, and it put to rest one of his deepest concerns.

Prophets just have miracles and signs follow their lives. They become a signpost for the people they serve. It's not that it is a faucet that is always on, but signs and wonders definitely help define the history of those they serve. Consider these instances when miracles followed the works of prophets in the Bible:

> *Elijah replied to the captain of fifty, "If I am a man of God, let fire come down from heaven and consume you and your fifty." Then fire came down from heaven and consumed him and his fifty.*
>
> —2 KINGS 1:10, *NASB*

> *Then the Lord said to Moses, "Pass before the people and take with you some of the elders of Israel; and take in your hand your staff with which you struck the Nile, and go. Behold, I will stand before you there on the rock at Horeb; and you shall strike the rock, and water will*

come out of it, that the people may drink." And Moses did so in the sight of the elders of Israel.

—EXODUS 17:5-6, *NASB*

The Lord came and stood there, calling as at the other times, "Samuel! Samuel!" Then Samuel said, "Speak, for your servant is listening." And the Lord said to Samuel: "See, I am about to do something in Israel that will make the ears of everyone who hears about it tingle."

—1 SAMUEL 3:10-11

Since that time no prophet has risen in Israel like Moses, whom the LORD knew face to face, for all the signs and wonders which the LORD sent him to perform in the land of Egypt against Pharaoh, all his servants, and all his land, and for all the mighty power and for all the great terror which Moses performed in the sight of all Israel.

—DEUTERONOMY 34:10, *NASB*

CLARITY AND DEFINITION—Prophets help define what God is saying to the people they are serving. One of the things Bob Jones did for the community of leaders he served was to make himself available. He helped scores of people comb through what God was saying or doing to them and what to do next with their revelation. He carried people's revelations with them and helped them to find a practical application.

If you had a prophetic dream, Bob helped you interpret it and make it useful. If you had a vision, he gave you descriptions and language for what it could mean. If you had a supernatural encounter, he gave you context.

Another friend of mine, Lance Wallnau, has a very strong prophetic gift helping advise people. You can tell him your spiritual journey and what you feel God is calling you to do, and he pops into wisdom, revelation, and insight. He homes in on a blueprint or helps you demystify or bring clarity to what God is saying.

IMPARTATION AND ACTIVATION—Prophets automatically activate others into the prophetic. It is part of what they carry. I have had the privilege of praying for hundreds of thousands of people for impartation. One of my favorite things is to hear the "before and after" stories—those people who hear from God regularly after the impartation.

The prophet Cindy McGill not only helps others interpret their dreams but also shepherds many people in receiving the gift of interpretation in their own life. Another one of my friends, Jerame Nelson, and his wife, Miranda, have a gift to release people into spiritual encounters.

As Jerame and Miranda pray for people, they have visitations and encounters with the presence of God. It happens with them wherever they go—in church meetings or when they are out and about with friends. They just carry the manifest presence of God.

The biblical city of Shiloh was the spiritual center for the Israelites before the first temple was built in Jerusalem. It was there that Hannah uttered her prophetic prayer for her newborn son, Samuel (see 1 Samuel 2:1-10). And then it was where the prophet Samuel gathered the prophets and where many were activated into the prophetic.

We also see the Early Church fathers releasing the manifestation of the presence of God in ways similar to what happened in Acts 2. Early Church leaders such as Tertullian and Origen walked in the same power and signs, which meant they prophesied, spoke in tongues, healed the sick, etc.

Let's now turn our attention to the roles God gives to modern prophets today.

9 | ROLES OF PROPHETS

The Bible records a very diverse, amazing array of people whom God selected as prophets.

As we look at the macro view of who were called prophets in the Bible, it will give you courage to embrace all kinds of people instead of just old white men with beards! Alongside that, on a micro view, I want to explore the nuances of some prophets and their words.

My hope and goal are to provide a context for the application of their words, what kind of people they were, and the outcome of their prophecies. This will then lead us into a "behavior profile" spotlighting a select number of prophets. In the Bible, some prophets were:

- male: Moses, Isaiah, Jeremiah, Abraham, Elijah, Elisha, and so on

- female: Sarah, Miriam, Deborah, Hannah, Abigail, Huldah, Esther, Anna

- children: Samuel (11 years old; see 1 Samuel 3:3)
- not followers of YHWH, or were non-Israelites at the time (e.g., Balaam, see Numbers 22)
- donkeys (see Numbers 22:28)
- related to other prophets: Miriam (see Exodus 15:20)
- guilty of getting their words wrong (Hananiah; see Jeremiah 28)
- started words by sharing their own opinion (Job's friends were guilty of this in Job 4–23)
- have unknown identities (see 1 Kings 20)

This list breaks the mold for what a prophet should look like. God is creative and, throughout history, has used men, women, children, and even animals to proclaim His word and Spirit to His children.

Prophets today are also racially diverse, come from different socio-economic backgrounds, have different talents and gifts, and have all types of family backgrounds.

TYPES OF PROPHETS

Let's consider some of the different types of prophets:

- Prophets to the nations (see Jeremiah 1:5-10)
- Prophets to the Church (see Acts 13:1-3)
- Identified as ancient prophets (see Jeremiah 28:8)
- Worshipers (see 1 Chronicles 25:1-7)
- Evangelistic (see 2 Kings 14:23-27)

- Prophets of justice (see 2 Chronicles 28:1-15)
- Prophets for business (see Ezra 6:14)
- Prophets for politics (see Daniel)
- Prophets for education (see 2 Kings 22:8)
- Prophets for consulting (2 Kings 22:14-20)
- Prophets as artists (see Ezekiel 4)
- Prophets as teachers (see Ezra 5:1-2)
- Prophets as intercessors (see Luke 2:36-38)

When you examine Scripture, you will see that more often than not, prophets were revered not only by those who believed as they did but also by strangers, foreign kings, and even enemies.

In today's society, the office of prophet has yet to emerge as God desires it. The Lord wants His prophetic nature to be taught and unveiled in all seven mountains of society (i.e., family, education, government, media, arts and entertainment, and business). As best as we can tell, in 1975 it was Campus Crusade for Christ founder Bill Bright, along with YWAM founder Loren Cunningham, who first put forth the biblical mandate of reaching these seven spheres. Nearly five decades on, we still have a way to go.

Indeed, the world will be a difference place when the office of prophet is restored and has dignity across industries, nations, cities, and spheres of influence. We must pray for a society where prophets are called upon openly before kings and presidents, businesses, churches, and schools—where the prophetic is sought in order to instruct and provide governmental words of guidance and foresight.

We see how powerfully God used His prophets in both the Old and New Testaments, and we have a society today that is longing for the supernatural. We must walk into God's mandate to help the world see that the prophetic is the natural bridge between heaven and Earth, and to make this happen.

And oh, what a beautiful sight are those who rise up and bring good news!

Second, as I have studied and thought about this subject, God has opened my heart even more toward the office of prophet. It is not limited to someone who speaks prophecies at church. Prophets are in the arts, painting masterpieces that completely reshape our view of beauty and creativity and of what God intends to show on the earth.

Prophets can be appointed by God solely for the purpose of bringing forth the sounds of heaven in song writing and worship. They need never preach but may sing the songs of God on Earth, in church and in society. Also, many of the Old Testament prophets were writers, some of whom we never heard a spoken word, but we read their words every day when we open our Bible. God appoints people to be writers.

By diving more deeply into the subject of modern prophets, it made me think about how prophets operate in our lives in so many different ways.

SIFTING WHEAT FROM CHAFF

I remember seeing a false prophet minister in Kansas City. He was really just financially motivated and used the appearance of the prophetic to get to people's hearts and wallets. He was brilliant and charming—and didn't know the first thing about the love of God.

I remember asking some of my Christian friends who regularly attended his meetings and contributed to his ministry if I could share about him. I told them that I believed he was a manipulator and not actually operating out of a biblical foundation.

They were so mad at me that they didn't talk to me again for a long time. Sadly, they sacrificed our relationship because of loyalty to this ministry. Several years later, he was exposed when some members of his team came against him and opened up the ministry to an audit. Not only did the organization not survive due to the rampant misuse of finances, but also he is now a teacher in the New Age movement.

Why can't otherwise God-loving, wonderful people see through the lies of a false prophet? One reason is that false prophets genuinely can be charismatic, fun, entertaining, and even spiritually gifted. They just aren't plugged into the right source.

A false prophet is simply someone who is trying to prophesy out of their own agenda for their own purpose. It could be someone who thinks they are doing good but do not have a connected relationship to Jesus as their source. They can even be a professing believer but they don't adhere to the theology of obedience in their relationship with God. They can have many other agendas and many other sources where they get their revelation, or they might just manufacture it.

I've come across several sophisticated false prophets. What I mean by that is that there are some people in the church who are exploiting Christians for money, power, and influence by using their revelation—or the appearance of it—to gain something.

Beware of the false prophets, who come to you in sheep's clothing, but inwardly are ravenous wolves.

—MATTHEW 7:15-16

The Bible warns against false prophets who claim to speak for God but who actually deceive the people they purport to inform. King Ahab kept 400 such false prophets in his retinue to tell him what he wanted to hear (see 2 Chronicles 18:4).

WHAT DEFINES A FALSE PROPHET?

If we flip-flop the definition of an authentic prophet, then we can easily determine the definition of a false prophet. A true prophet of God will be committed to speaking God's truth and will. He or she will never contradict God's revealed Word, written or spoken. Micaiah speaks the confession of a true prophet just before his fateful confrontation with Ahab: "As surely as the Lord lives, I can tell him only what my God says" (2 Chronicles 18:13).

In contrast, a false prophet is not appointed by God. They speak pleasing words instead of words from God. They speak words to benefit themselves instead of God. They might even prophesy in the name of other gods. Some prophesy in the name of the Lord but they do not speak His words.

That is why God has given us the Holy Spirit to help us know truth from deception. This precious gift, given to God's children thousands of years ago, is so powerful that many seek its use for personal gain. Much of the New and Old Testaments is filled with stories of false prophets and those who come with an antichrist spirit. To be clear: not everyone who "misses it" on a prophetic word is a false prophet. We are human vessels through which the Holy Spirit speaks.

It really has to do with the heart. Ultimately you can tell if someone is a false prophet or teacher if the core of their words doesn't consistently reveal the love of Jesus. If there are all kinds of agendas but no trace of this central theme of Christ's love, then they are false. To not have love means to not have Christ. (Please read the section on accountability of a prophet.)

JUDGMENT PROPHECY

The effects of sin were seemingly instant in the Old Testament because God's Spirit was not resting on or abiding in man. No payment for sin was situationally present. The animal sacrifices only provided a temporary atonement for sin and a foreshadowing of Christ. That is why instant judgment was provided; anything antichrist in thought or deed needed to be removed.

Uzzah the Levite was helping escort the Ark of the Covenant for King David and was killed instantly when he tried to steady the Ark as it traveled toward Jerusalem (see 2 Samuel 6:7). Hananiah, the false prophet who led the people to believe lies, was executed after Jeremiah told him he would be punished for his sins (see Jeremiah 28:12-17).

Even prophets of God received instant judgment when they sinned. Prophets had multiple layers of responsibility because of the words they received. If they spoke incorrectly when the Lord's Spirit was resting on them, then they would be misrepresenting God. This was no doubt sin, especially when the eternal word of God was being formed in them and their life's story.

Here's a broad statement that will offend a few people: Most of the prophetic people who give words of judgment have been inaccurate. Very few can produce a pre-recorded message from the event, but they'll try to claim the glory of it in hindsight: "I told my team about this one night," or "I knew this would happen."

A lot of people who give judgment words have never taken the responsibility to track if they happen afterward, so it's hard to build accountability and a track record of trustworthiness. (We will go into this more later in the book.)

I have been around some wonderful prophetic people who declare judgment, and then when others ask them later why it didn't come to pass, they claim, "People must have prayed." This response implies two things:

1. It was a word of warning, not a guaranteed occurrence, so they should prophesy it that way (if at all). There should never be a time when someone tells a region, city, or person that God will judge it/him without hope. God will allow the consequences of sin at times, and this is often misinterpreted as His judgment.

   God is not in the business of bringing disaster or calamity directly to people who have made bad choices. It is obvious that the wages of sin is death and that when you make a bad choice you will reap at some point from it. God will, however (according to Scripture), protect His covenant with His people. He will move on behalf of the poor, the widow, and the orphan; and He will oppose people who violate children.

Sometimes Christians who prophesy earthquakes, tsunamis, droughts, and more are, in actuality, declaring that God—who loves and sent His Son to bridge the gap relationally—needs a reoccurrence of the price paid to make these things not happen anymore. In other words, "Because you, too, are separated in sin, you have no hope of redemption, so I have to destroy you. Jesus doesn't count for you because you rejected Him too." That is a very sick gospel.

2. This prophecy was conditional, and pointed out basically what people would reap based on their current sin. Spoken biblically, such a prophetic word would need to inform them that they had a chance to repent and avoid those consequences.

The conditions of any judgment prophecy need to be defined and then tracked.

Number two is a huge one when people are declaring what God wants in their church, city, region, etc. They *have* to be accountable in defining the terms. God is in the business of speaking in ways we can understand so that we can then change and be transformed by them.

Is the prophet saying that because we have alcoholism over our region, God has to burn our crops by March 1 (a true story about an African prophet's prophecy that never happened)? If the word doesn't happen, did that alcoholism rate change in a trackable way? If you can't track it, then it's not worth saying—because it makes God look like a crazy person!

All negative (judgment) prophecies should have a redemptive perspective or else they are just not aligned with the nature of God.

Let's imagine you give a word about a storm hitting because of sin, an earthquake happening because of corruption, etc., and the disaster occurs. If you can't define what has changed because of the word, then what is the word about in the first place? God doesn't just point things out; He loves the world and wants to transform people, not kill them off because He's mad at them.

There will be a day of judgment when everyone who doesn't choose Jesus will face Him. This has been prophesied in the Bible (see Romans 14:10-12; 2 Corinthians 5:10; 1 Peter 4:5). Because of the nature of the Old Testament and the promise of the final judgment, many Christians apply judgment words or theology to their prophecies.

Prophetic words in the New Testament, other than the biblical revelations and prophecies of the book of Revelation, were never judgment based. Even with Ananias and Saphira, Peter didn't prophesy judgment—he just knew they were coming under judgment as the Holy Spirit judged their hearts.

John 3 talks about this:

> This is how much God loved the world: He gave
> his Son, his one and only Son. And this is why:
> so that no one need be destroyed; by believing
> in him, anyone can have a whole and lasting life.
> God didn't go to all the trouble of sending his

Son merely to point an accusing finger, telling the world how bad it was. He came to help, to put the world right again. Anyone who trusts in him is acquitted; anyone who refuses to trust him has long since been under the death sentence without knowing it. And why? Because of that person's failure to believe in the one-of-a-kind Son of God when introduced to him.

—JOHN 3:16-18, *MSG*

BIBLICAL APPOINTMENT OF PROPHETS

It happened in fourth grade.

It was the first time I was not picked by the "cool" team to play dodgeball. I ended up playing on the "dorky" team and we got creamed. (On rainy nights, I think I can still feel the sting of a dodgeball hitting me smack in the small of my back.)

In God's prophetic order, His faithful servants never lose—He wants to choose you for His "team" to speak words of redemption and salvation to a culture dying of spiritual thirst.

So, what are the requirements for being picked—or appointed—by God to be a prophet? Let's take a look at a great example in the book of Acts.

"Brothers and sisters, choose seven men from among you who are known to be full of the Spirit and wisdom. We will turn this responsibility over to them and will give our attention to prayer and the ministry of the word."

This proposal pleased the whole group. They chose Stephen, a man full of faith and of the Holy Spirit; also Philip, Procorus, Nicanor, Timon, Parmenas, and Nicolas from Antioch, a convert to Judaism. They presented these men to the apostles, who prayed and laid their hands on them.

So the word of God spread. The number of disciples in Jerusalem increased rapidly, and a large number of priests became obedient to the faith.

—ACTS 6:3-7

What qualified these men to be appointed? Four key qualifications are mentioned (though I am sure there were more):

1. They were men of good repute (or moral character and standing).

2. They were full of the Spirit of wisdom.

3. They were full of faith.

4. They were full of the Holy Spirit.

I don't know about you, but these are the exact types of men and women I want to be appointed as prophets in my church or organization.

These were characteristic traits they walked in well before their day of appointment. Also, they were validated in their calling based on the fruit of their lives. In other words, unlike my fourth-grade dodgeball game, the choices weren't random or based on who happened to be considered a "cool" kid that day.

We see the outcome of Phillip's appointment in Acts 8:26. I believe Phillip was now identified (called out by God and man), appointed (positioned), and imparted (empowered with spiritual inheritance and authority) to walk out his calling. He shows us the fruit of this appointment by evangelizing the Ethiopian eunuch, performing miraculous signs of transportation, and evangelizing in every town along his way. Wow! He was bearing a lot of fruit.

Now *that* is what a person looks like when they are walking in their appointed office.

THE ROLE OF THE APOSTOLIC WITH THE PROPHETIC

An apostle is someone who is called to build the structure in the church or an industry where the Holy Spirit can come and reside. They are a person who builds kingdom government, culture, and strategy in the world.

Many apostles are recognized over church and ministry movements, but not as many are seen over entertainment, politics, business, etc. When you are qualifying who an apostle is, you are looking for someone who isn't just building the local or micro work, but someone who is broad and big-pictured.

Prophecy, prophetic ministry, and prophets work beautifully in the local church and marketplace, but some prophets are called to operate in a higher way. Such prophets have a calling to build the kingdom in the macro, not just the micro; the trans local, not just the local.

When someone begins to have a prophetic calling over an industry, nation, or ministry movement, God will always bring them into alignment with an apostolic leader. The two offices were made to work together. Though a prophet can be extremely independent, in my studies of even current ministers, there is always an appointed apostolic relationship when there is a commissioned prophet. This is a biblical model: In the New Testament, apostles and prophets worked together to build the foundation of the structure of early Christianity.

And because God's Word, both the *logos* and the *rhema*, is just as active now, the same apostle-prophet couplet works today.

Kris Valloton, a prophet aligned with Bethel Church in Redding, California, has done powerful kingdom ministry because of his connection to Bethel. I think of Paul Cain and the relationship he had to Mike Bickle, the leader of the International House of Prayer (IHOP) in Kansas City.

I think of Lou Engle and his connection to Che Ahn and HIM Ministries in Pasadena. I think of Kim Clement and the relationship he had with the apostolic leaders of TBN and GodTV. I think of Lonnie Frisbee and his relationship to both Chuck Smith and John Wimber.

I think of Cindy Jacobs and the relationship she had with the late Peter Wagner. I think of Joy Dawson and the relationship she has with Loren Cunningham. I think of Bob Jones and the relationship he had with Rick Joyner out of the Morningstar constellation of ministries in North Carolina.

These are some of the more visible prophet-apostle alliances, and of course, there are thousands more across the earth, on every continent. I wanted to just touch on a few to help lay out a spiritual grid for the case that prophets work best in relationship when aligned with an apostolic base and framework.

I can also think of dozens of prophets who don't have a relationship with an apostolic person or base, and how their fruit is much less graspable.

God has designed these roles to work together, but I think there is a temptation for prophets to be independent. This is because many of them are also builders, teachers, and reformers, and may have an apostolic bent. It is so easy to live in the grace of just a teaching ministry, prophesying, or being an inspirer, without coming alongside or under the structure of an apostolic ministry or organization.

Either the prophet doesn't come under because of relational pain or fear or they are just not called to be in this type of fivefold model of ministry. In such cases, they don't have the need for this type of relationship and are instead in relationship or under the authority of a local church or ministry team.

As we move into Part II of the book, we will transition from looking at the theology of prophecy and the prophetic into the personal growth process of your prophetic journey.

PART II

SELF

10 | THE GROWTH PROCESS

One of the main reasons I am writing this book is to help bring mentoring, tools, administration, and growth into your prophetic journey.

One of the top questions I am asked is, "Will you mentor me?"

What a privilege it is to be asked! But of course mentoring is a huge responsibility and a decision not lightly made. Also, most people are looking for more than a little guidance, opportunity, and impartation. They are looking for access to the gifts they are inspired by to come through the person they are asking to be mentored by.

Here's the reality: you already have access through the Holy Spirit, and growth has to be a very personally driven process in your life. I love how Paul reminded Timothy to fan into flame the gifts he had received through times of prayer and the laying on of hands. The verse doesn't say, "light a fire, Timothy, and then stand back while I fan your flames."

159

In other words, "God gave some gifts and we helped you get started, but you are responsible to stoke the fire of passion that leads you into your spiritual journey. No one can want what you want as much as you are supposed to want it."

If I begin to mentor you the old-school way, you go everywhere with me, watch me, and sometimes participate with me. In this case, you will definitely have a good time (because I am loads of fun!), but it doesn't guarantee that you will grow in your gifts.

By hanging out with me, you might even be sacrificing some good growth time where you are the one being activated. Instead, you are doing a "ride-along" with brother Shawn, kind of like in the back seat of my prophetic ministry travels. I have rarely seen someone who is being mentored by just serving and shadowing a prophetic person actually gain the same amount of authority and prophetic impact as someone who is directly pursuing the gifts.

This doesn't mean we don't need mentors or that we shouldn't spend seasons serving. But we need to do it in a way that is still in direct pursuit of what we want to be mentored in. For example, you would never do a residency at a hospital after years of college and be satisfied just answering phones at the front desk.

You would never do an art mentorship without actually painting and getting critiqued. It is the same in the prophetic: if you want to grow in it, and you want a mentor, make sure it's a direct, hands-on process.

The majority of your growth in the prophetic can be self-managed. In other words, you can practice daily, learn to apply the prophetic in your life and the world around you, and compare your process with your peers.

Also, you can find tools, books, conferences, seminars, and online groups to help nurture your process.

But most importantly, if you want to grow in your prophetic gifting, spend time in God's presence. Pray, yes, and read the Word. But also sit with God and listen for His voice—rather than just talking to Him. Sitting in silence—practicing solitude—can be tough! But it's worth it.

If you want to grow, here are the three biggest steps to consider:

1. Track everything God is saying through you or to you for a season. You can transcribe, journal, record—whatever enables you to listen or look back so that you can weigh what you said. Even get rid of filler words you used, or lesser themes that are just nice encouragement. Find the meat of what you are saying.

2. Write up your testimony/life story, and say it out loud, focusing on the times when God showed up, how He encountered you, and how He has led you (or is leading you). Focus on all the key points of your history of what God has said or showed you that have changed or formed your direction, focus, or plans.

3. Write what you believe God is speaking to you about your destiny and calling. Write out the sphere of influence you feel called to (you can use the seven-mountaintop model if you need a template). Write the types of people groups you are called to love. Write the skills, talents, gifts, and spiritual gifts He has given you (or is going to form in you) to accomplish this calling.

This process will help you to identify what He is saying to you in a very deliberate way, as well as teach you how to see the prophetic in your own testimony and story. It will also give you a grid for what God has called and destined you to do. You can use these tools as a foundation for pursuing the prophetic.

THE EQ AND RELATIONAL INTELLIGENCE OF A PROPHET

Prophets in the Old Testament were labeled as abnormal or sovereign, but they were also allowed to be weird, violate relationships, and not be accountable to social standards.

Things have changed so much since the last book of the Old Testament, Malachi, was written some 2,400 years ago.

We now have the Spirit of God, who has helped us develop a sense of psychological maturity worldwide. He has infused the Christian culture with life skills, emotional intelligence (EQ), psychology, self-help, true biblical studies, and theology.

In other words, today we have a move of self-empowerment that creates healthy identity. It checks prophetic people at the door for their understanding of emotional and relational health before giving them a platform. Today we can go way past the weaknesses and excesses of Old Testament prophets. These days we are seeing a generation of prophetic Christians ready to hear the voice of God and share Him in powerful ways.

Paul wrote to the Corinthians about a very key prophetic principle: "The spirits of the prophets are subject to the prophets" (1 Corinthians 14:32, *NASB*). We use this verse a lot when we expect prophets to be orderly and honoring to the spiritual atmosphere in the room, but this verse actually goes much further than that.

Paul is urging prophets to pursue self-management, self-awareness, and personal accountability to the crowd or community to which they are prophesying. Too little is spoken on the governing of the prophetic, but that is because the whole Bible gives a relational framework to the gifts—one that prophecy is supposed to adhere to as its core value system.

Paul and the New Testament writers had no desire to separate ministerial roles from the full accountability of the core message of relationship. A single role—such as missionary, prophet, or pastor—was talked about in the New Testament no more than two or three times. Our main identity as a son/daughter and co-inheritor with Jesus, however, is a central thread throughout the New Testament.

It's essential to focus on the majors instead of the minors. When we make our identities the central theme of prophetic ministry or the pursuit of the prophetic, it gives prophecy the same importance as every other gift of God's. It's so important that we hold prophetic ministers and people who prophesy accountable for their relational skills and not just their prophetic words.

RECEIVING FROM GOD

Surely the Lord GOD does nothing, unless He reveals His secret to His servants the prophets.

—AMOS 3:7, *NKJV*

God wants to speak to you—and not just so that you can help others. It's about the way God made us: the concept of speaking is to share our nature with someone, to give of ourselves, to open a flow of relational connection. The prophetic gifts only reinforce this.

I love the Gospels because they provide examples of how Jesus was trying to connect very personally to individuals based on the Father's love for them. Sometimes we get so caught up in trying to be like our model, Jesus, that we forget to be ourselves—the way He made us!

Yes, we are made in His image, but we can get very caught up trying to receive His words and interpret scripture so that we can effectively reach others. It really starts with us and how He made us, and then having Him work through us.

God wants to speak to you about your life and help bring context to what He is doing in you. If you can interpret God for yourself and hear God about your circumstances, then you can easily give out of the overflow of that to others. So many people get this backward and think that they can't hear God for themselves.

As a matter of fact, Gordon Lindsey, who used to document healing evangelists from the 1950s, made several statements based on his observations. He found that many of the people he was tracking found it hard to hear God for themselves.

I think this was because at that time, there was not a strong culture of relationship and personal connection in the Church, and the emphasis was about outward ministry, to the detriment of personal growth and the ability to thrive inwardly. It's like the expression "you can't transmit what you don't have."

It takes vulnerability to hear God for yourself, to hear what He is saying about your present and past. It is one of the beautiful ways that Christians can experience great growth though, as we hear what God is saying about our history and life. He wants to deliver messages to us about who we are—who He destined us to be.

I think of Peter in Acts 10 when he was caught up in a place of worship. God took him into a trance, which, as we discussed in chapter 6, is a heightened state of spiritual awareness. This word "trance" in Greek is *ekstasis*, which represents an ecstasy that is also described as amazement and glory. Peter had a connection with God that transcended his normal mental and emotional state. In Acts, Peter's mind is filled with so much wonder!

In this state of *ekstasis*, Peter received a word of knowledge through a vision. He was supposed to go minister to a people group outside his sphere of Jewish culture. It was a change of direction, of theology, and of paradigm, but his heart was filled with love for these people. Even in the midst of this incredible experience, Peter began to doubt what he had seen.

In His perfect ingenuity, God gave a Roman centurion named Cornelius an encounter with an angel who gave him a word of knowledge as well. The angel told the Roman to go and find Peter, the tanner. He even showed Cornelius where he could be found!

This is radical and beautiful! God changed Peter's paradigm, but not just for his ministry. He wanted to make Peter's life exponentially richer and fill it with greater purpose.

We are called to hear from God for ourselves in very specific ways. You are your own best personal prophet because Jesus lives in you. He will confirm what He has said to you and through you, but so many times it will start with you—even words of knowledge.

The goal is not information; it is love. But practically, how do we develop receiving? We will develop this theme all through the next section in many different ways.

MAKING WORDS USEFUL: RECEIVING AND CAPTURING PROPHECIES

I first want to present a simple model for processing personal revelation.

Back in the 1980s, Mike Bickle helped raise up a handful of prophets who became notable through his church, the Kansas City Fellowship. Because he was open and excited about these prophetic men and women, there was a lot of prophetic revelation that started to be shared, especially by the ones he recognized as prophets.

Mike was always looking for practical ways that words from God could be administered into the life of what he was building. He and the prophetic community that he led in Kansas City came up with a very simple model that I think is still very helpful today. It is a three-step process:

1. REVELATION—Getting the message from God

2. INTERPRETATION—Getting understanding for what the message, dream, encounter means

3. APPLICATION—Getting the application for how to administer it into lives or the organization

One of the things Mike teaches leaders is that though they might not always receive the revelation, they might be the one to understand how to apply it once it is inter-preted. He teaches that God spreads these three roles amongst a body of believers at times so that there is in-terdependence within the community, instead of depen-dence upon just the prophet.

This simple model always sets my expectation; so if I receive a revelation, I can pursue an interpretation and then an application to make it useful.

A MODEL FOR STEWARDING WORDS FROM OTHERS

You know you do it: you receive a prophetic word from someone and then you lose it. You toss it in a junk drawer, forget to make a note of who gave you the word, or can't remember the voice of the person you recorded on your phone.

One of the most valuable things I ever learned in my relationship with God is how to steward my prophetic words from others—and equally as important, how to or-ganize the words I receive from God for myself.

I have heard about many models on how to do this, but one model doesn't necessarily work for everyone. We all have different needs and learning styles, and we use, store, and recall information differently. So, I want to present a few ideas that might help you develop your own system or starter model for capturing and keeping prophetic words.

When receiving a word from someone:

RECORD YOUR OWN REVELATIONS AND WORDS. Keep a journal or notebook by your bed or use your phone as a recording device. Use it to capture thoughts, revelations, dreams—whatever you can—all in the same place.

A friend of mine asked God for dreams, and for several weeks she had amazing dreams. She never wrote them down, though, or had them interpreted. She became discouraged when they stopped and asked God why. She heard the Spirit say, "You didn't steward what I gave you, which shows that you actually just want the experience but are not willing to let it lead you."

This made her realize that she had a stewardship responsibility. It's similar to when you open a piece of mail that requires action, and you tell yourself you will respond later. Then you never do. Similarly, if you wait until a later time to get basic interpretation or application for a prophetic revelation, then you may not return to it. Sometimes emotions and feeling come with the revelation, and unless you capture the experience in the present, you may lose the full impact of the word if you wait.

ORGANIZE WORDS GIVEN TO YOU. I can't emphasize this enough—part of good stewardship is collecting the information and knowing where it is. Keep track of it! Give yourself easy access. If it's a recording, keep it in a file where you can hopefully compile a list of recordings over time. If it's a written word or email, keep it accessible, somewhere you can find it if you were looking. Some people transcribe their words all into one file, some keep a journal, while others keep the recordings on their phone in an application. No matter how you do it, keep a record (and a backup).

LISTENING PRAYER. When you receive revelation or get a word from someone else, it is good to have a regular time to read it or listen to it. Clear yourself of all distractions, spend a little focused time by reading the Bible, then ask God a question. Now wait in a meditative way. This means, don't let your mind wander. Center your thoughts on Jesus. Don't let them wander. Then think about the question and ponder it in your heart. Try this for 2 to 5 minutes per question and ask 1 to 3 questions every day.

APPLYING WHAT YOU LEARN. Learn how to see or apply what you hear to your life. As you start to hear more and more from God, determine any measurable steps you need to take based on what you are hearing or receiving. If the revelations are perspective builders, acknowledge that so that you don't look past the budding gift that is growing. I would say that a good portion of what you receive will develop more out of the growth of your inner life than steps you might take in your outer life. Notice themes, and write them down.

FEEDBACK FROM FAMILY AND FRIENDS. Run the prophecy by someone who cares about you or is part of your spiritual journey. Send them a copy with the subject line "Pray with me about this and tell me what you think."

REVIEW YOUR PROPHETIC WORDS MONTHLY. Spend one of your devotional times monthly or bimonthly with your spouse, mentor, or a friend you are tracking with spiritually. Track with each other on spiritual things that God is showing you, review any new words you have received yourself or from others, and share your heart about them. Then pray together about their interpretation or application.

REVIEW YOUR WORDS ANNUALLY. Go over all your words annually, especially the ones that have not yet been answered or fulfilled. Look at long-term words from years past, as well as current words. Do some listening prayer. Let it be a personal prophetic "summit time" where you allow God to form some big-picture ideas or even just refresh your thinking about what He is saying.

ASK LOTS OF QUESTIONS. If you aren't getting revelation, don't assume God isn't talking. He loves to hide Himself so that you can come find Him. He loves the chase and the intimacy it builds.

WHEN THE HEAVENS ARE LIKE BRASS. If I hear nothing when I am praying, I ask God the following five things:

- What do You love about this person most right now?
- What do You want to say about their relationships and/or friendships, and what are You doing there?
- What are they spending their time on—is it a job, career or hobby that You love, God?
- What is their spiritual calling?
- What are good secrets that would reveal Your God nature to them?

Notice that I start with the love of God and the person's heart. The old prophetic movement always started with a person's calling, which is really not where the prophetic should usually start.

God is always a connector of heart before purpose. Look at the woman caught in adultery in John 8. Jesus did not enter the scene and say to the men about to stone the woman to death, "What is this woman's purpose in life?" Instead, He went straight to the heart issue.

After writing something in the sand, He stood up tall and said to the woman's accusers, "Let any one of you who is without sin be the first to throw a stone at her" (John 8:7).

The men quietly slipped away until it was just Jesus and the woman. Then He spoke to her heart, saying, "Woman, where are they? Did no one condemn you?" She said, "No one, Lord." And Jesus said, "I do not condemn you, either. Go. From now on sin no more."

I love this verse because Jesus doesn't lecture her on the wages of sin, her lifestyle, or other secondary issues. He simply tells her that He doesn't condemn her, and to go and sin no more. Straight to the heart—that is our model!

Sometimes we don't hear God because we don't ask Him what *He* wants to talk about. We assume we know and so we ask the wrong questions. When praying for someone, the first question isn't "How can this person serve You, God, and make You happy?" It's a wrong identity question for the prophetic. Our questions should all start with "What are Your favorite things You love about this individual?"

FAITH = RISK

And without faith it is impossible to please God, because anyone who comes to him must believe that he exists and that he rewards those who earnestly seek him.

—HEBREWS 11:6

Faith and risk are synonymous. If you are going to grow, then you are going to have to try new things that sometimes are scary or do not make sense.

When do you stop risking? When it doesn't pay off at all—over and over. I had a friend who used to try to get words of knowledge about people's names. He tried and tried but it never worked. He invested so much of his effort that he actually let his genuine prophetic gifting and focus fall by the wayside.

There is a balance between trying to risk and being practical enough to do what you are good at. I tell people to risk privately for a season and see what the fruit is. If it doesn't work, then I suggest trying again in a year, or sooner if they have grace to try. In regard to honing your prophetic abilities, I am talking about trying it dozens or even a hundred times before you give up.

People have asked me, "When did you know you were good at hearing people's names?" First of all, I never think I am an expert in receiving words of knowledge; it always feels risky. Second, I tried probably close to a thousand times and only got a few names right before it started to connect in me. And even then, it only connected through a revelation encounter—but I think my faith made room for the encounter. I don't think I would be operating in the prophetic if I hadn't qualified to God that I was willing to be faithful in risking.

Sometimes it may not be just names you hear prophetically. It occurred to me while I was in South Korea that God knows the Korean language. (Brilliant thinking on my part, right?) I asked Him to show me things in Korean, and you know what? He did! First, He gave me a few city names that people lived in as part of a series of words of knowledge for them. This was amazing, but I thought I could have heard those before, so I kept really pressing in.

Another time I was in Vacaville, California, and was in that place of being half awake, half asleep. I heard a man's name and a date and saw that he was married to a Hispanic woman. Then I started to type three lines of Spanish. I don't speak, read, or write Spanish, even though I am a native Californian and resident. You'd think I would at least know some Spanglish, but no—I barely understand any Spanish words (which shows how illiterate I am with foreign languages).

I was afraid to take the risk, but I asked if there was a Jeff in the meeting associated to a date. There was a man named Jeff, and the date I shared was his birthday. I asked if he was married to a Latina and he was. Then I had a Spanish-speaker come up and read what I had written.

It wasn't just a mixture of Spanish words I had heard; it was three coherent sentences. Basically, the message I received said, "Estoy bendecido por tenar una madre como tu. Eres una madre a todo dar. Como tu no hay nadie." The interpretation was said to be, "I am so blessed to have a mother like you. You are a totally charged mom, a way cool mom. There is no one like you."

Then I began to prophesy how the wife was a high-powered woman, but soon after marriage she had four children in a row and had to channel that high-powered business ethic into motherhood. She was learning to embrace motherhood as being just as important, if not more important.

I said to her, "You could have been someone in the business world; you have rubbed shoulders with great business leaders. You have met John Maxwell, haven't you?" and she had. Then I said, "All your kids are champions and will accomplish great things, but it takes a champion to raise one. One day your kids will say what I just wrote to you and be so grateful to you."

We were all so blown away and felt God's love for her!

I also love this story, involving a social security number:

> I was sitting with a couple who came up and asked for prayer after a meeting. I had never met them, and they had a beautiful mixed-race marriage. They shared that they were having some problems and asked me to pray to hear from God for them.
>
> As I prayed I heard a number: 525-63-9403 (this is a made-up number for illustrative purposes, of course). I didn't want to say it out loud because it was just on the edge of my imagination; it could have been revelation, or perhaps it was just my imagination.
>
> In either case, I could feel God's love for them, so I took a step. "Does this number mean anything to you?"
>
> "That is my brand-new social security number! I just became a citizen of America!" the husband said, blown away.
>
> I prophesied, "I know this was probably a very hard process with lots of problems." They both nodded. It had been very difficult to get status. "It's just like the problems you are going through right now. They are hard, but God has your number, meaning that if God cares about your citizenship, then He cares so much more about your marriage and lives. You are going to make it through this in amazing ways." They felt so loved, and even though I didn't solve their problem, they had new hope.

RISK-TAKING

Be emotionally intelligent and understand your environment, but by all means try new things.

God's imagination is huge and will inspire you to do things you would have never thought of on your own. That is one of the purest indicators of when I know it is God—it's something I would have never thought of, and it's not just a repeat of the last thing I did.

God is so exciting and creative. He uses the prophetic to create images and snapshots of His love that we will re-watch in heaven more often than kids watch reruns of their favorite cartoons.

Think about how Jesus spat into mud and smeared it on someone's eyes. Jesus received a word of wisdom about this unorthodox way of healing the man's blindness (see John 9:1-17). Can you imagine if your pastor did that the next time he prayed for someone at church? This approach would never enter into a normal human's mind; but Jesus, full of the Father's heart, saw this and did it!

Jesus is our great example of how to listen accurately, because He never did any two miracles or gave any two messages the same way. There was always a new and deeper part of the Father's heart to reveal.

BEWARE OF PATTERNS

I see spiritual boredom come when people attempt to re-create their prophetic success over and over. The problem with this, for example, is that you might see that someone's favorite color is blue and interpret that he is going to grow in revelation, but this may not mean the same thing the next time you see blue. Maybe it was the color he just painted his room, and God wanted to show him how much He cares because He knows it was his late-father's favorite color.

If you get stuck in thinking you can do direct interpretation, then you might miss the nuances of God's great and extravagant creative love. We are creatures of habit, but God is a creature of depth, and there is no end to discovery.

Challenge yourself! If things start to get easy for me, then I ask God for more and try to take risks that are hard for the stage I'm in. I got so used to hearing people's birthdays that I started to ask God things like, "How about the city they were born in, or the hospital name?"

God loves this! He wants to reveal way more than we can imagine. He loves when we challenge ourselves to really see into His heart about His desires. He is the one who wanted to speak to you before you ever wanted to be spoken to.

REWARDING RISK

In our local church and friendship environment, risk should be rewarded, not just success. It takes a lot of courage and faithfulness to keep trying to prophesy or give words of knowledge. Picture it as being more of an athletic training.

When I was learning how to prophesy, we had an old-fashioned church directory with names, phone numbers, and sometimes addresses. I made it my goal to call seven to fourteen people a week for almost two years so that I could pray for them and try to encourage them. We had thousands of members, so I never got through the whole directory. But I learned every day from my time of prayer ministry with them. After a few hundred calls, I had collected some skill in starting the conversation, ending the prayer, connecting what I was seeing to their hearts, etc.

Growing in the prophetic takes time and practice.

11 | LIFE WOUNDS AND PROPHETIC WOUNDS

I had a friend who was trying to meet his birth parents and was carrying some deep father wounds. During that time, his whole filter was one of fathers wounding their children and abandoning them. Sometimes he would give prophecies through this filter, along with some very real encouragements.

After getting feedback about ten times, he was able to see that the father wounds he was perceiving in others weren't registering and had nothing to do with others and everything to do with his own process. He began to back off of these sentiments while in prayer ministry times and to focus more on what was important to them. As a result, his prophecies were more accurate and helpful each time.

Each of us carries wounds from our past that can distort our present. It could be a father or mother wound, issues of injustice we are sensitive about, or ideals that have been oppressive to us. The list of possible wounds is deep and wide.

Sometimes when we are ministering we might go to that wound without really realizing it, as that is where our humanity leads us. However, it is not where God wants to go. You may have wounds that God wants to heal, but He doesn't want you to transpose them onto the message He wants to give someone else, causing the revelation to be distorted or blurred.

I have seen people who are really affected by racism bring that into the majority of their prophetic ministry, not as a civil rights leader, but as a bitter person who uses the prophetic to try to bridge the gap of their current wounding. On the other hand, I have also seen the prophetic heal racial issues. There is a difference.

I have seen people with terrible marriages trying to prophesy about marriage issues when God was doing something entirely different. They were fixated on the issue of marriage because of their own wounds. Of course, I have also seen God use the prophetic to heal marriages in ways that other tools could not.

Getting our internal world right will help us see God more clearly and accurately in our external world. When we have life wounds, we have to let God and our community take us on a journey of self-awareness. By finding healing from past hurts and wrongs, we can still be effective—even while on a journey toward wholeness.

Some areas of pain go away, but the scars are still there. In this case, we might see the world in that area through a specific filter of what we have experienced. If that is a factor, then it will definitely extend into your prophetic ministry.

I am sure you have seen people who form bad theology because of unresolved pain (e.g., someone who believes all alcohol is bad because they were raised in an alcoholic home). Or they believe all entertainment is the devil's because of R-rated and inappropriate media. Our personal biases can distort the revelation of a prophetic word if we do not continue to surrender ourselves to God's leading.

The more self-aware we are, the more we will set aside our personal goals, issues, personality defects, wounding, or hot buttons from our ministry time. We may not be over everything from our past, but God's presence isn't limited to our weakness, and His strength is inside of us.

PROPHETIC WOUNDS

If you have been wounded by prophecy, or someone used the Bible in a way that hurt you, I am sorry, deeply sorry, and God is too. People get wounded over the prophetic in a few ways:

SOMEONE USES PROPHECY TO MANIPULATE OR CONTROL SOMEONE ELSE. They prophesy in order to get the person to do what they want them to. For example, "You can't date that person because I have a concern about them; God has shown me." Or, "You are not supposed to move." Or one of my favorites, "God has shown me that you're ambitious and want a promotion because of pride."

I have heard story after story where someone steered those who would listen through prophetic words instead of relational community. Prophecy is supposed to support community and even define seasons and times, but not define the relational psychology or culture of the community itself.

Community is defined by love, a culture of honor, and a respect for others' differences. When prophecy is used as the primary driver, it will violate freedom of will and choice and will steal the spotlight away from love. It will cause people to be performance-driven and competitive in unhealthy ways.

Prophecy is always a support gift for relationship, not a control gift to manipulate relationship.

SOMEONE IS NOT TEACHABLE OR ISN'T OPEN TO BIBLICAL CORRECTION WHEN THEY GIVE AN INACCURATE WORD OR ONE YOU DISAGREE WITH. I remember someone giving me a terrible word about a sickness they felt I was going to experience. I told them, "I don't believe that is true and I don't believe God is going to allow that. I am sorry you feel that way."

They responded, "This is now the judgment of God because you are not receiving from one of His prophets." It was so weird and so religious to think this way! I never contracted that disease they prophesied that year, and this so-called prophet isn't even walking with God anymore.

Can you imagine if I had trusted him and started to partner in a religious journey of fear when this person didn't even have longevity in their relationship with God?

SOMEONE GIVES YOU A WRONG PROPHECY AND NEVER TAKES RESPONSIBILITY. This is a hard one and can occur when you are hoping for something to come to pass and it doesn't. It is painful when someone you respect hears from God for you, and then it doesn't bear fruit. This can cause a wound as well. When prophets track well, however, there can be more of an opportunity to heal, because they can apologize. Either way, it still hurts, and part of your challenge will always be to keep your heart as open as possible toward the gifts of the Spirit.

SOMEONE PUBLICLY HUMILIATED YOU BY PROPHESYING INAPPROPRIATELY IN FRONT OF OTHERS (WHETHER IT WAS TRUE OR NOT). I remember pointing at a lady at a meeting and saying, "God is touching your marriage and things that have been hard are going to get better." What I didn't expect is that everyone became extremely concerned about her and her husband, who had gone through a really difficult time years before, but the marriage was now fine.

It made people suspicious about the health of their marriage and it took her months to undo the damage caused by my insensitive prophecy. A few years after, she came to me and explained what had happened through it. I felt terrible, and the experience caused me to never be the same.

When people point out negative things about someone else in front of others, the ones listening may not make it all the way to the positive part of the word! Psychologically, we are geared toward negativity, so it is hard when someone says something in front of others that can be labeling or even disrespectful.

I am much more careful now when I have a sensitive "hard season" word to share with a person. Such prophecies should be shared confidentially. At the time, they may seem innocent, but the backlash in the community or with their friends might be quite difficult and damaging.

This is not to say that such a sensitive prophecy might not be true. This scenario is not about being right; it's about acting appropriately and stewarding the word with relational intelligence and emotional sensitivity. A prophetic word that is delivered in private can take on a whole life of its own if shared in public. The stakes are so much higher in front of others—delivering God's revelation to an individual is an honor, and we need to recognize and exercise biblical order in how we prophesy.

I do want to offer you some encouragement: If you have received a wound from any of the situations listed above, or other unlisted mistakes people have made, don't hold the gift responsible!

The prophetic is a beautiful set of spiritual amplifiers of God's love. Don't allow yourself to shut down your openness to prophecy because of misuse or someone else's mistakes.

Go on a journey of fighting for health!

WHY SOME PROPHECIES DON'T COME TO PASS

If you are like me, you have had some prophetic words that just didn't happen. You may have placed a great deal of hope and trust in the revelation, only to be let down after years of silence. It can be so discouraging when a prophetic word does not happen. It can cause us to question our ability to have faith or others' ability to hear from God for you.

It leaves four choices for you to believe:

1. You sinned, fell short, or blocked God's blessing.

2. The enemy is attacking you and won (or is winning).

3. God changed His mind.

4. You or the person who heard didn't hear God correctly, or the word was off.

Because the prophetic involves humanity, it is so easy to get frustrated with the process. Most people will not believe the prophet is off, so they will judge themselves, believe it was the enemy, or get mad at God. One of the reasons why it is good for prophetic people to track their words is so that they can be aware of their accuracy rate. Of the four choices above, number 4 is the easiest to accept because forgiveness and healing can take place more quickly.

As humans, we have this desire to quantify everything. For example, when we are in pain, we have this need to understand it and be able to articulate it. I have found, though, that oftentimes when a word either has not come or was a bit off, there is no easy answer for why.

Why did God allow someone to prophesy and set your hope that way? What is wrong with that person, God, or you who believed it? I would say that there are times you have to forgive, release, and let go without an explanation—but don't turn a blind eye. Get wiser because of it! Not jaded, not bitter, not arrogant, but wiser.

I had a friend who felt he was going to marry a certain person for a number of years. She finally got married to someone else and never really felt he was the one for her, even when they dated briefly. He was heartbroken because how do you answer the question of what happened? Was he super deceived and never actually heard from God? Maybe.

Did she fail in her ability to hear from God and exercised her free will—which God won't violate—to marry someone else? Maybe. Did the enemy cause problems? Maybe.

But for my friend, there really was no way to understand exactly what happened. From then on, he did become more careful when he thought he heard something from God about the future. As well, time did heal his heart.

He hasn't become self-suspicious, because he grew in a more deliberate prophetic journey. He now tracks his prophetic words, measures fruit, and does his due diligence before taking bigger steps of faith.

I am happy to say that he is now married and has no regrets. He realizes that he wouldn't have even wanted to marry the other woman now that he is happily married. Interestingly, he never had a prophetic word about marrying his wife—he just fell in love with a godly woman!

I think this is so powerful.

The bottom line is that sometimes we will see through the glass darkly—we don't know why some things in the prophetic realm don't come to pass, but we do know that God wants to speak to us. The amazing thing is that even though we may not know the why during hard or confusing times, we still get to know God, and He will heal our hearts.

What happens when someone gives you a wrong word, judgment word, or a word you don't want? Don't receive it. It is as simple as that. No one can curse what God is blessing.

I had a man tell me that I wasn't called to ministry but was pursuing it out of my own selfish ambition. You know what I did with that? Nothing. I thanked him for sharing—but didn't thank him for the word—and moved on. It had no power; I didn't need to rebuke it or him, and I knew I would never see him again.

When someone gives you a prophecy you can't shake, give it to God and don't let it label you, predict for you, or dominate you. That is not what prophecy is for.

On the other side of the coin, what do you do if you prophesy a word that someone either doesn't receive or rejects altogether? People should be able to reject your word without rejecting you, and vice versa. If it's about relationship, we have to be honest with each other. If someone doesn't believe in your gift, your prophecy, or your prophetic word, it shouldn't take away from basic human-level connection.

THE IMPORTANCE OF PRACTICE

I really enjoy my level of gifting and partnership with the Holy Spirit these days, but it wasn't always that way. I experienced more than a whole decade of trying to hear God that was very frustrating at times. I would constantly feel like I didn't have enough access to the gifts in a way that satisfied my pursuit. I also felt like I wasn't connecting with the same kind of anointing or quality I was hearing from some other people's manifestation of the gifts.

I grew up in a Christian home with parents who loved the Holy Spirit and welcomed His presence in any and every situation. They modeled the practice of the gifts not only to us as a family but also in the home groups, classes, and ministry teams they shepherded over the years.

My father was in the Air Force, so one of their favorite things was to launch a home group for military men and see God change their lives through encountering His Spirit. Prophecy played a key role and my parents were never satisfied staying center stage. Rather, they always activated everyone and empowered them to prophesy, pray for healing, speak in tongues, and practice the spiritual gifts. It was a very empowering environment.

My parents included us in directional decisions and would ask us to pray to hear from God with them. Many times, they would have a couple of options of where my dad's military orders would station us, and they included us in the decision. My mom encouraged us to pray about the friends God would give us on the next base and to ask for revelation about them.

We just practiced hearing God all the time and included Him in all the big decisions. When we lost things, we would pray for God to help us find them. Sometimes He would give us a word of knowledge about their location. A few times it was miraculous and we just would glory in the fact that God was so real and loved us so much.

What I learned from my parents' very healthy perspective on God is that if you want the gifts, which are freely given by the Holy Spirit, then you have to practice them. You have to be deliberate and pursue them.

As you step into the prophetic, you won't even really know what you are doing for the first few hundred words you give (yes, I just said *few hundred*). It is the learning time when you get as much out of the process of prophesying that the people might get from receiving your words. You are learning language, spiritual connection, how to translate what you are hearing/seeing, delivery, and process.

When I first started to take my growth in prophecy seriously, there weren't a lot of visible practice areas. We had a ministry team on Sundays, but that was pretty much it. I was hungry to grow though, so I made it a goal to prophesy over one person a day. Most of the time I failed in my goal, because I didn't put any plans in place to succeed.

Then I set some goals rooted in planning. I determined to prophesy over one person a day at least five days a week. Right after my devotional time I would pray over the church directory and try to single out someone. I didn't know most of the people, so it was weird to call them. Now we have email, which takes out so much of the risk (thank God), especially for those of you who are growing. The stakes felt high, but I would prophesy to these people, right over the phone!

After giving hundreds of words over a few years, I started to really draw connections between the spheres and situations for which God had given me a passion and anointing. I found my lane when I prayed for business people, creatives, families, and entertainers. I would add politicians as well, but that came way later for me.

It was amazing after that learning process how I could discern God's heart quicker and with more meaning. It was because I had applied practical experience to get to know the gift and how God uses me in it. After my first ten years, I started to enjoy the moments of feeling like the gifting was easier to come by. As well, prophecy started to be my "go to" for simple things like filling out birthday cards or graduation gifts (I would buy a natural present too, but I couldn't help but pray into a word as well).

It was in my face in celebration moments like anniversaries. I couldn't help but encourage friends to pray with me when they were going through hard times and we would do listening prayer together.

In other words, if you set a path to grow, you will. You might be in a church that has great support for this, or you might not even go to church right now. Perhaps you are stationed in the military in a far-off country, are on a job in a remote location, or are in a hospital recovering from sickness or surgery. It doesn't matter where you are; you can grow in the prophetic. But you have to set goals, then make plans to move forward.

God will never say no to something that He set as a framework for you.

> *Whatever you have learned or received or heard from me or seen in me—put it into practice. And the God of peace will be with you.*
>
> —PHILIPPIANS 4:9

It takes hundreds—if not thousands—of attempts at public speaking and teaching before you become decent and relatable, and that is if you are doing it in an educated way. But for some reason, we expect people to prophesy as experts in their first seasons of trial! But it just never happens that way in a context that can be maintained.

We can create an atmosphere of growth by doing the following: track words, share failures, celebrate successes. Also, it's important to remember:

- When it feels like you have given somewhere between 30 and 50 correct prophecies, you will receive a useful amount of feedback. At this point, you can begin to see where you have matured and where your authority lies. When you give 500 to 1,000 accurate words, you will start to be a trusted advisor in that area. When the number eclipses 1,000 to 2,000, you will start to gain a reputation of credibility outside of your current environment.

- Establish a trusted prophetic relationship with a local community such as a home group, church, or ministry school. Sometimes people tell me, "My church doesn't offer prophetic ministry." That is true of a large majority of churches, but in almost every region—or even online—you can find a supportive community that can help you grow. In your community you can start to track, share failures, and celebrate successes.

THE PROPHETIC JOURNEY OF LIFE

"Build history with God and He will build history through you."

— BILL JOHNSON, LEAD PASTOR,
BETHEL CHURCH

As you build a history of accurate and connected prophetic words, the world around you will begin to listen to you or look to you. To be more specific, people will begin to look to God in you to bring transformation to their issues and lives. Once you start to build an accurate, measurable prophetic history (including a trackable list of prophetic words that came to pass), you will begin to grow in long-term influence.

Of course, there will always be new people and groups to meet and connect with who won't know or relate to your history. But building a track record in one sphere helps you to have boldness in others. Seeing God through your history will cause you to be more confident, take greater risks, and believe for more.

Hearing God and seeing the fruition of your words are infectious, because you see that these gifts and your relationship to God make a huge difference in the world around you!

Compare notes with friends who have had inspiring journeys to find out how God spoke to them and led them. Ask how prophetic words helped direct them and how their own experiences with God's voice defined their life opportunities and experiences.

We learn much more quickly when we see someone else's journey through their eyes. What God does for one is multipliable to many. Our podcasts and materials can definitely help you here as well.

Once you start to track with a community over someone's individual or corporate words, you get to celebrate their fruit. My close friends have consistently pointed out how much faith I built in them by pursuing huge visions over my life or by stepping out and prophesying over others.

It is so rewarding to be around others long term and share the testimonies of God's goodness. Part of celebrating fruitful words only happens in the context of committed community. Do you hear correctly and in ways that empower the world around you? Your family and friends will keep those celebrations about your prophecies living on.

12 | LEARNING TO RECEIVE IN THE PROPHETIC

Let's just say drivers here in Southern California are not always super courteous. But every now and then, a friendly driver emerges. Though many people won't use their turn signal to change lanes, or wave if you let them in front of you, some will.

Recently, I had a funny sort of "standoff" at a four-way stop sign.

I reached the intersection after another car, which was on my right. Here in the U.S., if you are the first car at a four-way intersection with stop signs, you have the right of way. So, I waited for the other car to go first through the intersection. But they just sat there.

I waved them through, with a friendly smile. They still sat there—and waved at me to go first. Eventually, after nearly thirty seconds of this (which feels like an eternity when you are sitting at a stop sign with a smile frozen on your face), I figured this person was not going to go first, even though they had the right of way.

In essence, the other driver had a receiving problem. Though it was clearly their turn to go, they just refused to move. In a way, it became a funny kind of "driving pride stand-off"!

Though this might seem like a trivial analogy, I sometimes see leaders, in particular, who have a similar sort of receiving problem when it comes to allowing others to minister to them. They are comfortable with "outflow" (e.g., praying for and helping others) but are less comfortable with "inflow" (allowing God and others to minister to them).

But a good amount of growth in the Christian life is having a childlike faith—of putting our pride aside, letting our guard down, and allowing God to minister to us as our Abba Father. Sometimes a leader might be afraid to be vulnerable, because (unfortunately) the Church has been known to "shoot its wounded." In other words, perhaps that pastor or prophet with a receiving problem did let their guard down, only to be burned through gossip or betrayal.

The fact is, however, that 50 percent or more of the prophetic is learning how to receive—especially learning how to receive from God. Alongside receiving from God, we need to learn how to receive from others. Receiving from others is an essential dynamic that God desires for all of us. The only way to receive openly, however, is to have trusting relationships. That is why finding a community that you can do the prophetic life with is so important.

Acts 2 is a perfect example of this. The spirit was poured out, everyone spoke to each other prophetically in tongues, and they were amazed about being heard and known. There was trust in the Upper Room that day—a community of believers who had grown very close through time spent together.

Prophecy is God's main tool for establishing His nature and plans for our close friends, family, and people we are connected with.

AN EASY MODEL FOR RECEIVING

GIVE HONEST FEEDBACK. If you are receiving the word, give the people who prophesied immediate feedback (perhaps not right afterward, but within a day or two). Make sure to share with them what really mattered in the word. If it is a word of knowledge, then let them know whether or not it was accurate, but do so in a positive, constructive way.

The more we share what is or isn't working with those who are prophesying to us, the faster they will grow. The prophetic is a skill set based on relationship, so it will only grow by relational feedback.

CONSIDER THE SOURCE. You should consider that you may or may not know their history with God and take everything with prayerful consideration. Just because they say something is from God or a dream doesn't mean it is, and it doesn't mean it is necessarily meant for you. Use your spiritual senses to discern from the word that is given to you.

Love should never be violated regarding receiving prophetic words from someone. Be available to give them feedback. If none of the prophecy landed, you need to communicate that to them.

LISTEN CAREFULLY. Try to draw parallels to what they are saying and your journey. Be open in your heart to see if what they are saying can confirm, edify, comfort or help you. Don't make it difficult or have a neutral face when they are saying something that is really meaningful. Don't make them jump through hoops; receive the word and the giver at face value.

RECORD WHEN POSSIBLE. As we mentioned in the previous chapter, this is one of the most important aspects of receiving a prophetic word. Value it by capturing it. If you don't have ready access to a recording device when the word is about to be given (i.e., the recording feature on a smartphone), write down as much of the word as possible immediately after you receive it.

Alternatively, if a third person is present, ask them to take notes for you. Otherwise, it can be difficult to hear what the Holy Spirit is saying as well as take careful notes yourself. After receiving the word, go over the notes; or if no notes were taken, immediately go someplace quiet to write down as much of the prophecy as possible.

I try to record the words I receive, as well as write them down. That way, I can hear the way the prophecy was spoken and listen to the inflection in the person's voice. And by having a written version, it gives me easy visual access.

As we discussed in a previous chapter, store your received prophetic words all in one place. Believe me, if you open your heart to God so that He can speak through others to you, you will collect a nice stack of words through the years. My words had been scattered for many years, so when I married Cherie, she missed out on seeing some of the beautiful history God had made by prophesying to people for me.

ASK QUESTIONS. This is also known as pulling out the fullness of the word: If you have the opportunity to ask questions, see if you can get them to expand on details. Ask them about things that registered with you and see if they have any more revelation about that point. Also, this would be a good time to ask about things you possibly didn't understand.

Gratitude. Thank them for spending time with you. It is precious when people will stop and listen to God on behalf of someone else. And because genuine prophecy is always voluntary, it is good to acknowledge the value of the revelation they just gave you and to be considerate of them. (Conversely, if someone wants to charge you money in exchange for a prophetic word, you can pretty much place them in the false prophet category!)

Follow up. If the revelation you are given is a foretelling word of knowledge, and the prophecy comes to pass, let the prophet know! It is *always* a blessing to follow up and bring the confirmation to the prophetic person. Even a one-paragraph email is going to greatly help them build a track record of faith and will encourage them to keep taking risks and loving people.

I highly value each time someone circles back with me after they have had a fulfillment or benefit from my prophetic words.

Also, if you are the person who brought the prophetic word, and you want to share the story with others, first make sure you have permission to do so from the person who received the word. Be sensitive to avoid a violation of a person's privacy, which can also damage your ability to be trusted.

Check the track record. Lots of people prophesy. Some even have ministries where they travel and speak domestically and internationally. Some go by the title "prophet"—and some actually are prophets. Be as shrewd as a serpent and as harmless as a dove before welcoming a new prophet into your group, church or organization (see

Matthew 10:16). Of course, if the referral is from a trusted friend or ministry, it is easier to say yes.

If you have any hesitancy or curiosity, however, it is fair for you to ask them about their accountability, track record, and network. Also, it's acceptable for you to inquire about their home church or community. Look into the fruit of their life and ministry. Ask their friends for a character reference.

If you are a leader and inviting them into your world to minister (whether church or marketplace), see if you can have a social time with them first. It can be as simple as a phone call where you share journeys, or if they are local, meet them for coffee before making a commitment to see if they would be suitable for your organization.

Why? Because it's very similar to letting someone you don't know babysit your newborn while you go out with your spouse. They have to be someone you have a basic relational trust for, or you are in for some potentially awkward times. Believe me, you don't want a charlatan giving a prophecy that is off, where you have to take the microphone and apologize on behalf of the "prophet"!

Pray about them; ask God what He thinks about them. Just because they have a prophetic reputation for others you trust doesn't necessarily mean they are a right fit for you or your group. I always think of referring prophetic friends the same way as I refer a therapist: not every therapist is the right fit for every person referred to them.

Each of us has our own chemistry, relationship needs, and trust factors for a person we would bring in for an advisory role, and prophetic people are no exception. If you have the opportunity, find out who they are before you allow them to exercise influence over your people.

If you have found someone to be credible and trust-worthy, allow them to share with you, your family, your team, or even speak to your congregation. Feel secure in what you built, and do not feel threatened. Their con-tribution should be in addition to what you have already created. Allow them to stretch you in your revelations and understanding of what God is showing you.

If you are a leader and inviting them into public min-istry and they are an outsider to you, you do not need to qualify every point to your congregation that stands out or is mystifying. Just focus on what God *is* saying.

TEST EVERY PROPHECY

Do not quench the Spirit. Do not treat prophecies with contempt but test them all; hold on to what is good.

—1 THESSALONIANS 5:19-21

Holding a prophet to the test is not a new concept, as it occurs throughout the entire Bible. God constantly held people to a standard and showed them what was best. In the Old Testament, people needed to trust the prophet and see if the word came to pass. If the prophet's word did not come to pass, then they knew it was not from God. In the New Testament, we find the same equation. The difference, however, is that the Church has a Helper, the Holy Spirit, who partners with us to bring prophecies about.

The contextual range in which a prophecy can be giv-en is very broad. Sometimes you will know right away that a word is from God, and sometimes you will be un-sure. That is why we need to test every prophecy and hold onto what is connected to us or fits within our interpretation for our own life.

It is not uncommon for a prophecy to be from the Lord but for the application of the word to be incorrect. For example, someone tells you that a dry season is coming to an end, and the person providing application tells you that you need to dig a pool in your backyard. The problem is, you live in an apartment. A more likely application would probably include a new season of productivity and fruitfulness—a new job, increase in ministry effectiveness, etc. (Or dig the pool if you want, but don't email me if your landlord complains!)

When pursued biblically, this process of prophetic testing and accountability actually helps build healthy relationships between a prophet and the community they are serving. Of course, as Paul talks about in 1 Corinthians 14, in all the gifts, especially prophecy, pursue them with love.

This should be an encouraging process, and every prophet should welcome it. If they are from God, they will invite you to put the prophetic word to the test, up and against the biblical guidelines for prophetic revelation. Don't receive words as your own until they have been tested.

Some of the prophecies I have received from a few very charismatic personalities didn't come true; I tested them and felt they were not God's word for me.

The following is a simple three-step model for testing words:

1. As the prophet is giving the word, record it or write it out. Take that recording and listen to it. See how it weighs in your heart.

2. Have peers and people who know you well weigh in on it: If it is challenging or exciting, make sure to bring it before some trusted peers. Don't just ask them if they think it's correct; ask them to prayerfully consider weighing it with you.

   Test the word against Scripture! This one seems obvious, but really put it to the test against the theology of God's goodness, how God speaks in Scripture, God's nature in Scripture, etc. If the foundation of the word doesn't take you toward Jesus, then I would question it.

3. Test the word against who you know yourself to be. Prophetic words can be confirmations of what God is already doing in your life. Do you keep a good account of your desires, dreams, and goals? God wants you to sift through the word and find the pure gold that lies within it. Sometimes, the kingdom of God is like a treasure hidden in a field (see Matthew 13:44). Will you go and find it?

As we learn to weigh prophecies—even if the words themselves don't enter into our prophetic journey—the process will help us evaluate our identity and purpose and will strengthen our resolve to believe what God is truly showing us. I have received directional prophecies many times that were just not from God, but the words did help me to stay focused on the direction God was showing me. These incidences even established more faith and clarity within me as I had to evaluate what I thought of those words in contrast to my direction.

WEIGHING WORDS AND GETTING FEEDBACK

Two or three prophets should speak, and the others should weigh carefully what is said.

—1 CORINTHIANS 14:29

Paul talks about how all prophecy should be weighed. What is this "weighing"?

One thing I have realized is that humans are prone to misinterpretation. We misinterpret things as a word from God when they are actually emotional responses to circumstances or hormones: "God told me I will marry you!"

We interpret certain scriptures for directions that *we* want to take—not God. We sometimes read into God's word, looking for confirmation for decisions, direction we are considering, and people we want to build relationship with. Because human beings are looking for validation, some things we take as prophetic might not be, and we have to learn to test our words.

Sometimes misinterpretation comes from desperation: "God told me I will get this job!" Then the job doesn't come, but we wanted it so badly that we claimed it by a desperation-based faith. Sometimes it's something we are hoping for: "We will win the lottery!"

Desire-based prophetic words are the hardest because they are oftentimes incorrect and can fill us with discouragement when they fade away, unfulfilled.

The good news is that we can create spiritual shock absorbers to help us withstand the emotional potholes and mental bumps in our prophetic journey. Paul talks about it in the verse above: As we learn to weigh carefully the prophecies we receive (either from others or from what we think God is saying to us directly), we will grow in our ability to separate our emotions and human desires from authentic revelation.

If we tend to drift into magical thinking (i.e., fantastical or exaggerated thoughts), we need to be especially diligent in allowing the Holy Spirit to be our filter. Simply put, we need to watch how we share prophetic words with others—especially if the person tells us their needs.

We have to weigh our personal and corporate prophetic experiences so that we can grow. But how do we create a workable system that doesn't become just one more responsibility that never gets done? The need is to find ways to stay balanced and not allow our emotions or weaknesses to get in the way of hearing clearly from God.

As a prophetic person, I am not just trying to see if I was right or wrong; I am trying to see exactly *how* right or wrong I was. Sometimes we ask people for feedback and they feel like it meant something but they couldn't define the full meaning for themselves. This shouldn't be a discouragement—you are learning to translate God! It takes awhile to be a good translator.

Think about a first-time natural translator who just started classes and how she is rated on her ability to accurately translate languages. After she is done, her teacher says, "You were eighty percent accurate in your effort." If the teacher is constructive, it shouldn't cause the translator to get discouraged; it helps her grow so that she can set a higher goal.

Sometimes we are only partially accurate. That's when we need relationally safe people with whom we are connected to give us a percentage of how accurate or helpful the word was for them. This can help people rate us realistically—in a kind way.

Learning to weigh the presentation, the heart, the anointing, the communication skill level, etc., can be daunting unless you take a relational approach. This is more of an artistic process at times than a direct science because it involves communication and the heart of God.

Weighing will cause you to grow though. Even when I am sharing a prophetic direction with my team, they may ask me, "How accurately do you think you're hearing God on this?" If I say, "Fifty to 60 percent," then as a team we will risk very differently on this issue than if I say, "Ninety to 100 percent." In other words, we start to weigh the revelation and communicate the efficacy of the word. Then we match it to the history of our other words and consider the fact that we are still growing in our ability to hear clearly.

One of my friends thought he was strong in the area of prophesying financial breakthrough. The problem was that it only happened a few times after he prophesied it would. When he started tracking his words, he realized he wasn't as accurate as he'd thought. On the upside, he learned how to tell the difference between a strong word and one in which he was not as certain. He knew he could take a greater risk when he had that spiritual connection than when he didn't.

Feedback is particularly important because:

- We receive advice concerning things that may be blind spots to us.
- We learn from the wisdom of others who are ahead of us on the journey.
- Our ability to communicate clearly what God

has spoken to us is sharpened.

- It provides confirmation of our prophetic insights that benefit us and those to whom we are ministering.

Through feedback, we can assess the degree to which our prophetic ministry is helpful. We can also ensure that there is no gap between what we have heard from God (regarding His heart and intention for a person and or situation) and what the person has actually perceived through our communication.

Feedback can come from:

- A person with whom we share a prophetic insight

- A leader, pastor, or spiritual oversight in the situation we are ministering

- A mentor or fellow team member

GETTING A WORD WRONG

In chapter 9, we discussed the subject of false prophets. Now I would like to discuss when an authentic Christian has a well-intentioned prophecy go wrong.

As we related earlier, in the Old Testament if a prophet spoke in God's name without His command, or spoke in the name of other gods, that prophet was subject to death. It sounds harsh, but if we see God's voice and nature as one, then we see how important it is for God to not let His righteousness waiver on the account of someone's opinions or presumptions.

Well, what does this mean for us today? Is there any room for error in the office of the prophet? What if a true prophet speaks falsely today? What if your friend tells you something prophetically and it doesn't happen? As a refresher from chapter 8, there are two main reasons why the consequences are not the same today as in the Old Testament: (1) the Holy Spirit, who serves as our guide and teacher, and (2) the forgiveness that comes through the price Christ paid on the cross.

With these two huge New Covenant qualifiers in mind, we can take a learning approach when we miss a prophetic word or are given one that is off.

THE HOLY SPIRIT IN THE PROPHETIC

The Holy Spirit helps us test the words we are given and guides us into their fruition. He helps us test their accuracy. He helps us test the accuracy of a prophecy and apply Hebrews 5:14 into our daily lives: "But solid food is for the mature, who because of practice have their senses trained to discern good and evil."

The Holy Spirit helps train our senses to discern if a word we receive is from God or human intentions, or even from another source. As we discussed in chapter 4, in the Old Testament the children of God did not have access to the indwelling of the Holy Spirit and only interacted with Him through prophets and leaders.

Martin Luther, the founder of Lutheranism and father of the Protestant Reformation, spent his life establishing that each one of us has our own relationship to God through the cross, resurrection, and the Spirit. We are justified not by a priest's faith for us or by a mediator, but through our own priesthood or relationship with God. If you believe that you are your own priesthood or justified by your own faith, that means you have to have your very own relationship with the Holy Spirit and that He will speak to you and train you.

> *But you have an anointing from the Holy One,*
> *and all of you know the truth . . . As for you, the*
> *anointing you received from him remains in you,*
> *and you do not need anyone to teach you. But*
> *as his anointing teaches you about all things*
> *and as that anointing is real, not counterfeit—*
> *just as it has taught you, remain in him.*

—1 JOHN 2:20,27

The word for anointing here in verse 20 is actually the same word that would be used for a priest who was consecrated by and filled with the Spirit. The word for anointing in verse 27 is actually the word for receiving an abiding from the Spirit of God. It is referencing what Jesus prophesied to the disciples in John 14 and 16, and how the Spirit would fill them, teach them, comfort them, and grow them in their spirituality.

Through our relationship with the Spirit of God, each one of us governs the destiny of our lives and the direction we are supposed to be walking in. In other words, in partnership with Christ, we are our own gatekeeper for what the Lord is saying.

If someone gives you a prophetic word that contradicts something God is telling you, then you are responsible for governing your life and not receiving the word. No one else can resist or reject a prophecy for you or govern your words for you. You have to remain focused on what God is saying to you and stay the course.

The same is true when you receive a positive prophecy: you have the authority to empower it in your life and help it take root and grow so that it can become fruitful.

MODERN PROPHETS

As we have discussed, the New Testament model for prophecy is radically different from what the Israelites contended with in the Old Testament. The people depended upon a priesthood—prophets and judges who were anointed this way; now we are all anointed individually in our relationship to the Holy Spirit. What an incredible gift!

FORGIVENESS AND THE PROPHETIC

The most overlooked aspect of what is different between Old and New Testament prophecies is simply forgiveness. In the Old Testament, if you got a prophecy wrong, you would be put to death. Today, however, if you get a word wrong, whether it's a sin or a simple mistake, you are given a heavenly relational option because of the price Jesus paid on the cross and the Christian virtue of forgiveness.

If you prophesy in the name of the Lord and get a word wrong, you are given forgiveness through Christ Jesus. The debt of your sin has been paid in full. You should continue a relational journey of repentance with the person to whom you gave the wrong word and learn and grow from that experience. Here are a few things that might help you if you get a word wrong:

- Change your approach toward the word; rethink what you heard to see if you missed a key element.

- Consider using more user-friendly language; sometimes we fall into prophetic jargon without realizing it. Not everyone knows what the leviathan spirit is or a spirit of Ahab!

- Pray into your words more before you give them;

unless the word is critically time sensitive (e.g., you have a dream about a friend in imminent danger, etc.), it doesn't hurt to bathe it in prayer if you are not confident about its accuracy.

If you forgive the sins of any, their sins have been forgiven them; if you retain the sins of any, they have been retained.

—JOHN 20:23, *NASB*

WHEN YOU RECEIVE A WRONG WORD

If someone gives you a word that is wrong, you have tremendous power from heaven—not the power of judgment, but the power of forgiveness. It is good that you forgive them. That is the option that the Holy Spirit will provide to you.

We not only receive forgiveness from God, but we also have the opportunity to extend it. If you are truly in Christ, then you can practice John 20:23: forgive the sins of any or retain the sins of any. What an amazing power we have in Jesus.

This doesn't mean you should blindly trust their ability to hear from God for you again. Whether or not they grow and improve in their ability to more accurately hear the Lord is a different matter. You have no obligation, in other words, to accept a future prophecy from them. Let the Holy Spirit be your guide. But by forgiving them, you will at least take the sting out of their mistake toward you by releasing them. It will also keep you from bitterness toward them or toward prophecy in general.

In no way do I want to minimize the pain you might be going through because someone gave you an inaccurate word that did not come to pass. I have received wonderful prophecies that never came to fruition. Surrendering such words of knowledge can be very painful. If a prophecy you received touched deep into your hopes or identity, the pain of it not coming true can cut equally as deep.

The process of forgiveness can be difficult if a prophetic person dealt with you falsely or gave you a word that damaged you or relationships. Though overcoming past wounds is not the focus of this book, I will say that the Holy Spirit wants to heal your heart.

Talk to God honestly and bluntly. Talk to your trusted team of brothers and sisters in Christ—those safe people who will listen to you and give wise counsel. Have your friends cover you in prayer. And if necessary, seek the help of a qualified Christian counselor who might be able to assist your healing process.

I don't know a single prophet who gets it right 100 percent of the time. Only Jesus was perfect in what He prophesied. I have had times when I've prophesied about future events with some detail and it didn't work out that way. In those cases, I had to go back and do course correction with the people to whom I prophesied. I don't think I sinned by giving them the prophecy (this is rarely the case when you are walking with the Holy Spirit). I was just trying to do my best to be obedient to what I was hearing, but I did make an error.

If someone has been off with you in their words, don't villainize the gift. Maybe the person who prophesied did not take responsibility for their error, but you can still forgive them and move on. Resist the temptation to judge the whole gift by one bad experience.

Ask God what He thinks about prophecy and open up your heart again. Prophecy is a lot like love: It can be perfect and deep with the right people. Some people don't understand it or they abuse it. We don't want to swear off love just because of a bad experience. Get back to a place where you feel you can love again and go experience love.

Just as committing a sin does not jeopardize your salvation in Christ, so too getting a prophetic word wrong does not disqualify you in the prophetic—nor does it label a person as a fallen or false prophet. We do need boundaries, accountability, correction, and growth, but all in the context of love.

13 | BUILDING CREDIBILITY, ACCOUNTABILITY AND AUTHENTICITY

Not all prayer warriors are prophetic, but I have rarely found a mature, gifted prophet who is not a prayer warrior. The thing about authentic prayer is that it takes time. And in our Western culture (at least here in the U.S.), time is seemingly hard to find.

The most accurate, fruitful prophets I know spend a good amount of time alone with God each day. Sure, they miss a day now and then, but the habit is in place. Like most things in God's kingdom, it's a simple equation, but not easy to do. I mean, raise your hand if you think spending *less* time with God will help you mature as a believer. Anyone?

So much of our devotional time is spent rapid-firing prayers without a two-way process built in. For generations, many Christians have not prayed in a way that leaves time or space for God to respond through His Spirit. We haven't set the expectation, and the current prayer world reflects that because it's a lot of quoting of scripture, rehashing the same prayers, and list praying.

In some ways, there is a beauty in the repetitive, contemplative pace of older prayers, but if you are not careful, it can become distant and mechanical. As with everything in the Christian life, it is about love and intimacy with the Father.

When you learn how to *listen* to God, it is because you have learned how to ask questions. You have learned to spend time in wonder, developing your spiritual curiosity, and to imagine what is going on inside of His deep heart.

As you grow in your relationship with the Father, you will grow in your ability to be an accountable, credible source of prophetic revelation.

ASKING THE RIGHT QUESTIONS

How do we learn how to ask the questions that stimulate answers? I used to be on prophetic teams that included people who were just gifted: as soon as we began to pray, they flooded with revelation. I would wait and pray and just not get it, meaning I was blank while they were full of words. I asked one of my friends what she did when she would blank out and she said, "I simply have a list of questions I ask God. I am very proactive."

This was one of those lightbulb moments for me. I was waiting for something to happen from God's side of the equation and failed to recognize that I have access to His heart and thoughts through His Spirit.

I began to create lists of questions to ask Him about people I was praying for, and it was so much more empowering! I had a new tool that worked like a checklist in my head; I could run down the list and it was a night-and-day difference in the interaction I was obtaining through it.

Some people are really good at going in "cold turkey" and just getting pictures, prophetic words, and ideas, but I needed a different process. I needed to be able to pray specifically. This hopefully will help some of you who are like me who just blank out during prayer.

Tools can be a great way to break out of a performance mindset and become more present with the gift of prophecy. Questions can serve as tools as you quiet your heart and ask God about the people, places or things you are praying about.

Here are some questions I have found helpful when praying for others:

- God, what do You love about this person?
- God, what do You love about their relationships?
- Is there anyone they love who You want to speak about? (husband/wife/child/friend)
- How are You blessing them or going to bless them? (financially, opportunity, relationally)
- What are they gifted in? (spiritual gifts/talents/career)
- What are their dreams?
- What are they hoping for right now that You want to speak about?
- How do You want to encourage their spiritual maturity?

Here are some more-specific questions:

- When is their birthday/anniversary/other special dates that are close to their heart?
- What is their favorite pastime?
- What is something they love that You want to show them You care about? (a pet, a hobby, a gift they gave)
- Who is their best friend?
- What is their favorite scripture passage?

BUILDING CREDIBILITY

Sometimes the words people give are minimized or not received well because the person has no credibility or is uneducated in how to build it. If you are giving a prophetic message to someone, credibility helps them as part of their weighing process. This doesn't mean that an unknown, unproven person can't give you an incredible word. Consistency, though, would cause you to view the person as credible because it takes some of the guessing out of the testing of the word.

Decades ago I prophesied over someone in a chat room. It was back in the day when we all just had usernames, and everyone stayed very shallow and anonymous. She sent a friend to me and said, "Can you do that same thing for her please?" I shared a prophetic message for the second woman, who ended up asking to call me. We had a powerful time of prayer on the phone and she accepted Christ.

A friend of hers called me on my phone who I didn't know. "So, my friend told me you shared a reading with her that really meant a lot to her. Can you do that for me?" Normally I would have said no; it felt very strange, but I could feel the draw of God. He loved this woman and wanted to speak to her.

I shared some very personal things and had some words of knowledge about her kids, dad, and husband. She was crying on the phone. She revealed herself to be the business owner of a psychic hotline based in Texas.

"Your accuracy is amazing! How you get to the heart is wonderful! Come and work for me! What is your percentage?"

I didn't know what she was asking. "What does that mean?" I asked.

"Your accuracy rate: how have you tracked it and what is it?"

I didn't have one. I didn't even know how to build it at the time as it was before I was tracking my gift. She explained how they tracked their psychics so that they could have proven credibility, and they had some who were up to a 79 percent accuracy rate.

I was fascinated and flattered, but I explained to her about my Christian foundation and how Jesus is my source. Then I basically took her through a sharing/teaching time about prophecy and the differences between what I was doing and what she was dabbling with. She asked many questions and ended up getting saved! Years later she is still walking with God and, of course, has shut down her psychic network.

I learned so much from her in that season. See, part of the reason why psychics are a thing is that they claim to have credibility. They spend time gathering people who will testify to their psychic accuracy. Of course, as Christians, we know that the source of their knowledge is not from God. It's a counterfeit. The enemy is predictable but crafty. He knows what people desire and will twist a beautiful gift like godly prophecy to his own advantage.

One test of prophecy is to ask, "Is this something Jesus would say—and is it the way He would say it?"

Credibility is critical for the prophetic people of God. As we restore the dignity of prophecy in all seven spheres of society (see chapter 9), we will need to reestablish the credibility of authentic prophetic gifting.

Do not neglect your gift, which was given you through prophecy when the body of elders laid their hands on you. Be diligent in these matters; give yourself wholly to them, so that everyone may see your progress.

—1 TIMOTHY 4:14-15

For this reason I remind you to fan into flame the gift of God, which is in you through the laying on of my hands. For the Spirit God gave us does not make us timid, but gives us power, love and self-discipline.

—2 TIMOTHY 1:6-7

Paul holds Timothy personally responsible for the growth and stewardship of his gifts and ministry. Likewise, we must steward the prophetic gift so that we may:

- honor leaders, especially through the tough times;
- submit to the process of adjustment and repentance when necessary;
- serve in the small opportunities;
- embrace the seasons of life;

- step out of our comfort zone (obedience) when a door opens up; and

- decide—over and over—to steward the gifts God has given to us.

HOLDING PROPHETS ACCOUNTABLE

In chapter 12, we covered what to do if someone speaks a prophetic word to you with specific, testable elements and that word doesn't come to pass. Now I would like to go a bit deeper into the process of prophetic accountability. Here are some key steps to take when course correction is needed:

1. Hold them relationally accountable in love.

2. Express to that person your past experience and inform them of what you heard them say.

3. Provide them an opportunity to respond.

Because prophecy can cover life and death and everything in between, our emotional construct is built on the words we receive. Why do we have to hold them accountable? Because our faith is built on relational principles and we have to take responsibility in love to give that person an opportunity to also take responsibility and grow from it.

I tell a story in my book *Translating God* that I think is so relatable on what happens when we don't take responsibility either way:

> In the mid-nineties, I went to a small group filled with really amazing young people I was connected to. I was supposed to speak, and a lot of them were really hoping we could do

a prayer time with the goal of hearing God. After I spoke I led them in a prayer, but I felt so blocked! I was asking inside, *what gives?*

I was looking for every external reason why nothing felt like it was flowing. I prayed God would change the atmosphere; I prayed we would have faith (meaning that *they* would have faith); I prayed against the enemy. I just kept praying things and nothing was working.

Then I asked God internally again, *why is this so hard? It feels like there's unbelief in the room.* Then I heard God, who was waiting for me to ask all along, say, "Do you remember when you prayed for that girl over there, Jessica, a year ago and you prophesied some things would happen in her life in a certain timeframe? They didn't, and she's disappointed in you and me. You never took responsibility, and what you are feeling is my desire for you to clean that up."

I was shocked. I was in a culture that usually blamed the person receiving the prophecy, rather than the prophet, if didn't come true. Wasn't it her fault if my prophecy didn't come to pass? Wasn't she responsible to steward her word and figure it out?

I think most people are like this, looking externally for blocks when sometimes we have created the biggest walls ourselves. I had really bad self-awareness at the time (and still do at times, but am building it intentionally), so God had to tell me. I didn't feel like it was my responsibility until I put myself in her shoes.

I had had a significantly known prophetic minister give me a word a few years before, which would have led me into a greater opportunity with more money and connections . . . and it didn't happen. As a matter of fact, the opposite happened for a while after that.

When I went to talk to the minister to ask him if he had insight on why the word hadn't been fulfilled, he was semi-offended and said it was probably because of something in me—that I was disobedient or in sin and had missed it. I was so shocked. I hadn't done anything consciously to delineate from my relationship with God, and I felt like I was advancing, not losing ground.

If I had believed what this prophetic minister said to me, I would have put myself in a penalty box or been marginalized in my faith. I would have been devastated if I hadn't worked on having a good solid identity and spiritual maturity.

I knew Jessica must have put a lot of faith in the word I gave her, and she was probably very disappointed. I looked at her and publicly said, "Did the word I gave you a year ago happen at all?"

She looked a little nervous and embarrassed. "No."

"I am so sorry about that. I don't know why some things happen and sometimes I miss it, but I want to take responsibility for that and tell you I am still growing. I hope you can forgive me and know I was just trying to encourage you."

She looked so relieved she got tears in her eyes. "Thank you!" And right then God came in the room. His presence of love came so powerfully I ministered to each person there, including her, and there was no block at all.

As people grow in their prophetic gifts, they need open and honest feedback. They need to hear how the word felt, how it sounded, what you understood about the word, how it was received, and what you think about it.

If someone wants to give you a word and they aren't open to feedback, then be careful receiving from them. Politely tell them you only receive words from people who are relationally accountable.

Prophecy is the beginning of a God conversation regarding a person, place, or situation. It is not a one-way street or a soap-box ministry.

Put yourself in a place of relational health where you feel empowered, edified, and strengthened with each prophetic exchange. It is your responsibility to put relational boundaries in place when needed. Just because someone comes to you saying they have the word of the Lord doesn't mean you don't have the ability to say no. Even the devil came to Jesus quoting scripture. Respond in love and just say no.

If you are in a community with leadership and someone speaks a word to you that you don't feel was right (or you are unsure), talk to your pastor, leader, or mentor. Discuss with them what you feel, what you experienced, and sort it out. There is a common saying that comes with the prophetic: "Eat the meat and spit out the bones." (If you are a Californian gluten-free vegan, "Eat the veggie patty and spit out the gluten.")

You don't need to adopt the prophecy as your identity. Examine it inside and out, look over the word, test it, and hold onto what is good. You are not denying God if you test your prophetic words. You are proving Him to be true in your life.

CONTROL IN THE PROPHETIC

Prophecy is a power gift. Some leaders and theologians would call it a sign gift. By this, I mean that prophecy is one of the "miraculous sign" gifts, along with speaking in tongues, the interpretation of tongues, healing, and working miracles.

While all of God's spiritual gifts have power, the sign gifts—including prophecy—contain a tangible, miraculous aspect to their power. Because the power of these gifts can be so dramatic and immediate (at times), they are readily open to abuse.

Let me explain further.

There is no doubt that when you hear from God from someone, it causes a respect toward them that few other things could. If someone said today that they were going to pay off your mortgage, what would your response be? Or perhaps you have a relative with a debilitating long-term illness and an "angel investor" tells you they are going to provide a new treatment and cure for them for free. In both cases, it would create an awe and respect in you immediately toward their heart and provision.

The prophetic is a gift that offers someone great benefit and creates loyalty and sometimes even a caregiver-type respect toward the prophetic vessel. Another way to look at it is that it wields the fear of God in people, as it should in the right context or balance.

The power that the prophetic gift, ministry and office holds should be revered and honored because it provides tremendous blessing for those who receive the prophecy's potential. This is one of the reasons why I am writing this book: to help bring balance and relational health to such a beautiful gift that brings so many benefits to us.

However, with great power and authority also come great injustice and misuse. All power or authority roles can turn codependent if the boundaries are not well defined. Because prophecy has been such a misunderstood subject, some people have been taken advantage of or been used, while others have controlled and manipulated.

If a person walks in a gift of God and exudes manipulation and control in His name, then run away very fast. If you are in relationship with them, then implement very strong boundaries until it is sorted out.

Also, if you are the person prophesying and someone tries to use you or manipulate you, run away. One of the main ways this happens is when someone comes up to you and says, "God told me you have a word for me," or, "I know you have a message for me." People don't realize how manipulative this approach can be. If not handled biblically, such a request puts the prophet in a tight spot, much like a psychic—they want information, and they want you to use your gift to get it.

If God wants to speak to someone through a prophet, He will. It's really as simple as that. God does not withhold good things from His children. I love the way Psalm 84:11

says it: "For the Lord God is a sun and shield; The Lord gives grace and glory; No good thing does He withhold from those who walk uprightly."

While God wants to speak to His children and walk us into our destiny, He is not an on-demand God. He is not our celestial Netflix, where we can order up a prophecy when and where we want. When I receive a prophetic word for someone from God, He does not need help with the process—neither does God respond to coercion and manipulation. Again, it is a heart issue.

As a prophet, I have a relationship with God that directs me to have revelation about certain people, events, and places—and I need to be free to pursue those. If someone is excited about my ministry and tries to hijack my time for their benefit in a manipulative way, then I have a responsibility *not* to perform.

I think we all have seen the person who, at the end of the preaching time, runs down to the front of the auditorium to jockey for the best position for ministry. Listen, I have no problem with someone being excited to receive a word from God. But when they knock other people down, or throw elbows like a basketball player? I know that sounds funny, but I have actually seen people rudely push others aside to get to the front!

These types of misguided approaches are some of the most common misconceptions and innocent manipulations in the prophetic. Typically, people who are uneducated in prophecy or the Bible can operate this way in ignorance. After all, it's exciting to be around people who believe they can hear from God and have a track record of accuracy!

It's only natural that people are going to try to figure out how to get the benefit of that for themselves.

The problem, however, is that they don't always start out with a biblical model or foundation for their spiritual hunger.

Another manipulation that can occur is when people prophesy words that would specifically benefit themselves: "God is showing me someone here has a car for me," or, "The Spirit of the Lord gave me a vision of a diamond ring that someone is to give." I was in a meeting when someone actually made these exact two requests, and yes, it made me cringe. (I am convinced that the prophetic is responsible for about 90 percent of the most cringeworthy moments in Christian history.)

Check your motives and, of course, you should never prophecy out of personal gain or selfish intention.

In contrast, a trap that is easier to fall into is when you try to "fix" someone or become their source of hope through prophetic gifts. This kind of codependent ministry will always end in tragedy over those relationships.

> *But whoever causes one of these little ones who believe in Me to stumble, it would be better for him to have a heavy millstone hung around his neck, and to be drowned in the depth of the sea.*
>
> —MATTHEW 18:6, *NASB*

Throughout modern church history we have seen very public examples of the misuse of prophecy. We had one man of God have a bad moment in the 1980s when he asked for millions of dollars on his popular TV show or else "God would kill him."

We had three very popular Bible teachers "hear from the Spirit" on when the rapture would happen. They stated the exact date and began announcing that everyone should get ready, for JUDGMENT WAS AT HAND.

We have had several TV evangelists ask for millions for their private jets or else the gospel would suffer. How about that single mom whose husband abandoned her, so she's now working two jobs to support her children? What do you suppose she thinks when she flips on the television and hears such a request?

PLAYING THE GOD CARD

Whenever you are ministering and you take away a person's free right to choose by saying, "God told me...," you are actually blocking their relationship with God. We call this "playing the God card."

A lot of this type of manipulation can be learned prophetic behavior or culture. In other words, some movements have embraced some of the excesses in skewed theology, while other groups are just not aware of their motives or weaknesses. Again, accountability is everything!

Finances play such a big part in our lives, and many prophets have been undervalued. It can be a real temptation to use the powerful language of speaking for the Lord to try to make financial ends meet.

I have also been around many current prophetic-type people who throw the God card on many decisions they make. The problem is, it's difficult to speak into something when someone says, "God told me to do it this way." If you do, you might be speaking against God.

When I was pastoring I had one lady who constantly moved around from home group to home group. Every time she didn't get her needs met, she would bolt to another group. I went to have a chat with her and asked why she had left her previous group. Her response was, "God told me to go to a different group."

We had a long conversation during which I realized she was dealing with a lot of emotional pain that just could not be adequately addressed in a small-group setting. Her unresolved wounds had caused a relational disconnection on a foundational level.

When I recommended she see a good Christian counselor, she was offended. "God hasn't told me to do that," she said. This was a kind of super-spiritual control masked as prophecy; it was a coping device for her and was affecting her ability to form lasting relationships.

This is going to sound like a very strong statement: Most people who manipulate the prophetic have a deep level of insecurity and low self-worth, so they misuse the gift to fill identity gaps. Such people probably have little self-awareness.

And sometimes they think a powerful word from God will provide them with identity or acceptance. If you have leadership over them, family relationship, or connection to their life, try to love them and show them their worth—but put up a boundary.

Another area where people can be manipulative is when they throw the God card on confrontation. I think people do this because the world is full of conflict avoiders who are looking for pain avoidance rather than conflict-resolution models. I have heard and walked people through so many stories where a leader tells someone, "God told me that you are doing this, and you need to stop," or, "God showed me this character weakness you have."

This just escalates what could be a teachable moment into a moment of crisis and fear. When a person feels like God is confronting them through friends, family, leaders, or other church members, it leaves scant room to process. They believe they just have to change, and a lot of learning goes away at this point.

In the above scenario, a person's motivation to change isn't based on their desire to grow in their relationship with God but because they are afraid of God. This unhealthy pattern does not lead to sustainable change but is oppressive and constricting.

It really comes down to legalism versus love—grace versus obligation. If you move legalistically, your goals may seem righteous when you use prophecy as the means to deliver change or correction to someone. The problem, however, is that you are going to risk violating relationship with them. Correction and accountability should be done out of relationship and proper authority, not governed authority from perceived leadership roles.

You should partner with God and invite Him into the process that you care so much about. Allow the Lord to speak with you regarding the matter *before* you discuss it with the other party. Please don't use "God said" language that takes away a person's right to respond out of relationship with you. If you do, then you are literally cutting off their spiritual legs in the situation. Don't take other people's power into your own hands.

THE GOD CARD—FULLY DEFINED

God should never be an excuse to violate someone or remove their ability to choose. Super-spiritualizing everything will lead to a violation of normal relationship. Even God gave people the choice to serve Him. Do not employ your prophetic gift to get your own way. The moment you say, "God said," you leave the receiver with one option: to accept what God said or reject it.

In the process, you remove their ability to challenge the prophetic word. Especially if they are young in their faith, what options do they have? Mainly you remove their ability to be in relationship with you. Rather, you have now foisted a position upon them where they have to relate to God *through* you. And that, right there, is not a biblical New Testament use of prophecy. To put it bluntly, it's spiritual abuse.

Traditionally, several denominations have employed Old Testament language in their modern expression of the spiritual gifts. I am not trying to dismantle denominational tradition, but I am challenging what can happen as a result of specific language used in manipulative ways— even if the manipulation is unintentional.

It creates an indisputable line in the sand when someone says, "Thus says the lord." What if the giver of the prophecy is wrong, or only got half of the word correct?

Since there was no liberty or ability to test the word, the receiver is forced to maneuver around a partially failed prophecy. And if the word is flat-out wrong, they have no choice but to reject the prophetic person giving the word. This eliminates the opportunity to have a healthy relational exchange in which they can explain to the word-giver why the prophecy doesn't fit.

The good news is that this type of prophetic train wreck is 100 percent preventable.

Several years ago, I watched one of our team members give a very specific word of knowledge to a woman at a prayer meeting. He said, "God has shown me there is going to be a healing tonight of your thyroid."

She said, "I actually just had my yearly checkup and everything looks great."

In delivering the word that way, he firmly stamped the situation "awkward" because he presumed she had a certain condition, but she didn't. Rather than tell her she had a thyroid problem (which basically boxed him in prophetically), he could have said, "Do you have a thyroid problem by chance?"

She would have then been free to say no, and his gift wouldn't have been challenged. But he went for it, and as a result, she had to reject the entire word. Because of his bad delivery, it jeopardized her faith in his ability to hear accurately from God.

Why do people throw down this kind of power language? Because it helps us feel like the word we are giving is more significant. It helps to upgrade the experience. When there is more presentation or drama in our language, we are sometimes taken more seriously.

Now, remember this is only a challenge in certain circumstances. I do believe there are times to share boldly what you believe God is showing you. But when you are in the early learning process of the prophetic journey, you need to tread cautiously. Boldness can increase with your accuracy and track record.

The reality is that you don't need to speak for God. He can speak for Himself to people around you. It is actually more powerful when God has spoken to you and you are able to walk into the word wholeheartedly and impart that to the receiver.

Have you considered why God gave the prophecy to you and not someone else? Not every prophecy is circumstantial. It is my belief that most prophecies are meant to build relationships or help someone become less self-sufficient and more relationally and God dependent.

At a minimum, the prophecy you give is for the building of relationship, which is one way we build up the body of Christ. This is one of Paul's definitions of healthy prophecy (and in the fivefold context):

> *And He gave some as apostles, and some as prophets, and some as evangelists, and some as pastors and teachers, for the equipping of the saints for the work of service, to the building up of the body of Christ.*
>
> —EPHESIANS 4:11-12, *NASB*

The Holy Spirit can speak to people directly, but God chooses to use someone else like you to give the message. God knows what you will represent in that moment in time to them—again, it's about relationship. The receiver needs you, who you are, what you're about, your giftings, callings, and love. You are the relational conductor that God has placed in their life, in this moment in time. Allow yourself to be seen, known, and heard.

If you hear from God and have a prophecy for someone, use language that provides them with options. Say things that point back to your process: "I felt something that might be from God for you," or, "I think God showed me." This also provides both parties with the best prophetic growth experience. As you process it later, you can learn what was right and what was wrong and grow in your gift and ability to hear God.

God cards should be the rare exception and not the norm. If you have a propensity to say, "God said," then you better have an amazing track record of hearing God.

Otherwise, you will leave yourself in isolation because of failed words.

In my relationships with prophetic teams that I run, we all are very careful to avoid using the phrase "God told me." In those very rare times when one of our trusted prophets does use that phrase, we really value and honor it and will even change direction because of it.

I learned to institute this attitude and culture from a church I was involved with in Kansas City, which did some radical course correction while I was there. I was on a team in a partnered ministry, and each week one or more of the team members said, "God told me." As a result, we were constantly changing directions and violating our five-year plan—not out of spiritual fruitfulness, but out of a fear of missing God.

We made very reactive decisions that left us feeling powerless on that team, and many people burned out. All their adaptive energy was drained down by whatever the main leaders' whims were in any given week.

Eventually, my senior leader told our whole team that we could only use the God card in a staff meeting once a year. It changed the whole culture of our meetings and so much more was accomplished!

In the final part of this book, we are going to explore putting into practice what we have learned in the first two-thirds of this book: How does the prophetic affect a church, ministry, or organization? What are the needed tools for implementing and activating a prophetic strategy in the lives of others? Let's take a look.

PART III

ADMINISTRATION

14 | NURTURING OTHERS IN THE GIFT OF PROPHECY

I have taught an innumerable number of people in some aspect of the gift of prophecy through the years. There are many ways to approach how one should go about nurturing someone in the gift. I would like to encourage you in a few areas I feel are most important.

BUILDING BLOCKS

People need to see a path so that they can walk on it toward a destination. The prophetic journey can be unplanned, spontaneous, and untethered, or it can be progressive, deep, and comprehensive. The teacher sets the model.

I like to encourage teachers to push in for more. Push beyond spontaneous inspirational words like "God loves you" and into life-altering prophecies that speak to the core of someone, where their heart is made bare and they feel known by God in an instant. See what is possible in the Bible and build until you get there.

A SAFE PLACE TO PRACTICE

Each nation has its beloved sport, whether it's cricket in Pakistan, baseball in the Dominican Republic, rugby in New Zealand, ice hockey in Canada, and football *everywhere else* (soccer as us Yanks say). All have one thing in common: If you don't practice, you don't make it to the big leagues. Period. Raw talent alone is not enough.

The same is true with the spiritual gifts, including prophecy: The more you practice, the better you will become at discerning, hearing, and conducting God's voice to a hurting world.

Practice, practice, practice. It's one of the most important things when it comes to relational gifts from God.

If you are a mature prophet and are mentoring others, provide them with a safe place to practice. Encourage people to be nonjudgmental and open about their prophetic experiences. Everyone can learn from one another. Lots of teachers think head knowledge is best, but this gift is an experiential gift—it needs to be heard, felt, and practiced more than taught.

It is important for you to clearly distinguish what prophecy is and what it is not. Show examples of both so that they understand.

GUARDRAILS

Have you ever bowled with bumpers along the gutters? Usually it happens at a child's birthday party. If you are not a very good bowler, it's actually pretty cool. Basically, it's impossible to make a gutter roll because the bumpers prevent the ball from skidding off into oblivion.

The same is true with beginning prophets: It is perfectly fine to provide guardrails—or bumpers—when teaching this gift. Start slowly and build up. For example, in the beginning stages it's probably not a good idea to let people prophesy dates, mates, and babies. They should grow into a trustworthiness and fruitfulness before they give those types of words. Be a father and mother to them by placing guardrails on their outflow until they are trusted and safe.

Keep their goals in check always. It's easy to stray from the goal when someone feels the weight and power of God as the prophesy. The apostle Paul said that he died daily. He kept his goals in check every day. How much more should we?

Teach them forgiving language. Encourage thoughtful language such as "I feel" or "I think I heard God." Using the wrong language can be very isolating for the giver and receiver. Emphasize the importance of giving your words the best possible chance to succeed.

If they say, "God said," then they are not giving themselves any option for missing even a small part of the word. New Testament prophecy should never be all or nothing. The giver should have options, as well as the receiver.

Everyone in the Bible is an example of what life is like when partnering—or not partnering—with God. Teach the core values of prophecy, including the biblical guidelines for a prophetic word, the gift of prophecy, the office, and its ministry outflow. Core values create opportunities and expectation. God loves when man plans his ways, because He will guide his steps (see Proverbs 16:9).

Prophecy is a relational gift. It needs to be understood and practiced around relationship. For many people, this is a new concept and they need to learn what it means to honor someone, listen to them, practice caring, and practice compassion. We can all grow in this gift if we give it a healthy place to grow.

SELF-AWARENESS

A tremendous amount of the gift is centered around the understanding of self. For each and every word we give, we are a huge part in its delivery, context, and connection. If we have poor self-awareness, then the words we give will be all over the place or unfruitful. Everyone should grow in their understanding of themselves with each and every prophecy.

How did it feel when God spoke to you that time? What impression was correct, which one was wrong? What thoughts did you consider when you gave the word? Every word should grow your self-awareness.

There is no failure, only learning. Teach a no-failure policy. Everyone succeeds if they simply did what they did out of love.

CREATING EXPECTATION FOR THE PROPHETIC

We have spent a lot of time defining what the prophetic can do for you. But how do you create expectation for the prophetic in the culture of your leadership, management, team, church or community?

Expectation is such an important thing because without it there is no contending and no faith—just a human type of hope that is a lot like wishing.

Think of the difference this way: When a couple is trying to have a baby, there is a wish, hope and desire for that potential future child. When the wife, however, actually becomes *pregnant*, the wish has now become an expectation. In a similar way, there is a significant difference between hoping that God will speak to your church prophetically and expecting Him to do so.

So, the question becomes: How do you move your church or movement from desire to expectation—to an atmosphere of *expecting* God to speak to you? When you make that paradigm shift within your organization, it alters the entire foundation of what you do and how you do it. Now you have an expectation wherein you *know* God wants to speak regularly, and each prophetic word from Him retrofits those foundations.

For example, it's no secret that California is a major center for earthquakes. Over the past 50 years—starting in earnest after the devastating 1972 Sylmar earthquake—the state has been retrofitting bridges and buildings to help these structures sustain a decent-sized earthquake.

In the same way, God wants to strengthen the structure of your ministry or church by building in an expectation for the prophetic. I love this passage from Ephesians:

> *Now to him who is able to do immeasurably more than all we ask or imagine, according to his power that is at work within us, to him be glory in the church and in Christ Jesus throughout all generations, for ever and ever!*
>
> —EPHESIANS 3:20-21

Now *that*, right there, is what an expectant church looks like! Paul does not say, "Now to a God who we kinda think might be able to do some pretty good stuff in our church..." Paul's expectation is powerful and palpable. And it's not built on wishes or hopes. The expectation that God is going to move in power is present and paramount.

I want to give you some ideas on how you can pray for and work toward this paradigm shift to replace wishing for expectation. Because one thing is for certain: God loves to speak to His children!

CREATING EXPECTATION FOR A CHURCH OR MINISTRY

CREATE A CULTURE OF CELEBRATION WHEN GOD SPEAKS. If the leaders are receiving prophetic words that move anything forward or help define the time and season, then share them with your team! Share how God spoke the word, what is coming from it, how it's beginning to manifest, and what you are hoping for. If you received a word that is helpful for your body or ministry to hear, incorporate it into your next message. Let their faith be built up by it.

GIVE SPACE FOR THE PROPHETIC. Initiate ministry time at the end of each service. One idea is to rotate groups of mature believers who can pray for the attendees for encouragement, healing, and help. If you already have a prayer time, invite the prophetic to come through your leaders and mature members.

Tell your team that at the close of worship you are open to hearing if they have a prophetic perspective, ministry direction, or word of encouragement for the church. Tell them you will share it by referencing them, or if you feel it is important for them to share, activate them and let them share it.

ENCOURAGE SPONTANEITY IN WORSHIP. Allow your worship team to be spontaneous in their worship at times and to sing out to encourage the congregation in songs, spiritual songs, or even hymns. Leading out a bit in worship during a spiritual flow can be a very bonding experience, and much prophecy can happen in this atmosphere.

THE PROPHETIC FROM THE PLATFORM. If you have some mature prophetic people in your congregation, plan for them to share from the platform either at the beginning or end of service. Allow them to bring a word or prophetic perspective maybe for the first five or last five minutes of the main message. Or ask them to share a word with someone during ministry time at the end to publicly demonstrate the prophetic.

INVITE PROPHETS TO YOUR CHURCH. Sometimes bringing in an outside perspective can be a powerful, positive step forward for a church or ministry. Each year plan to make room for authentic, mature prophets to bring a word to your church.

NURTURE YOUR TEAMS. Invite prophetic people or the prayer ministry team in your church to visit each department maybe once a quarter. Set aside time for them to pray for individual staff members and to minister to their needs. By creating an expectation of revelation in your departments, you will help unleash them into their full potential.

Setting a prophetic expectation takes one step at a time. Prayer, of course, is the beginning point. Then take one action step after another. To borrow from a beloved film, "If you build it [create room for the prophetic expectation], they will come [i.e., God's spirit of revelation]." Setting up a prophetic expectation really starts with including it and promoting it in your everyday ministry life.

Building a prophetic expectation for nonreligious organizations is much different but can still be accomplished. I have seen people do this well when there are Christians at the helm of most areas of the company.

SETTING THE SPIRITUAL CULTURE

Can you imagine being mentored by someone for three years—during which time they never made a mistake or committed a sin?

That is the way it was for Jesus' disciples. He appointed them to walk with Him for quite some time, but He did not expect them to be perfect before they could walk in their callings. As a matter of fact, Jesus knew they were not perfect and yet He still appointed them. As you read the Gospels, you see Christ's patience with His disciples. He establishes a clear, healthy balance between holding them accountable and loving them when they err.

One of the most powerful examples of course correction in the New Testament surrounds Peter's denial of Christ. At Jesus' darkest hour, Peter abandons Him; but the amazing part is that Christ prophesied to Peter that he would deny Him three times—and he still did!

Despite this, what does Christ do? He goes straight to the core values of the Gospel: love and forgiveness. After the resurrection, He reinstates Peter into his full apostolic role by reversing each of the three denials by asking Peter three times if Peter loves Him (see John 21:15-17).

So, Jesus models a healthy balance by confronting Peter, but in a way that does not strip Peter of his dignity. He knew His disciples were very human people walking out both their successes and their failures, and He gives us the ultimate model of course correction.

Spiritual culture is guided by a church or ministry's core beliefs. Everyone should have a set of beliefs that they can hold firm to. This would be your nonnegotiable set of beliefs, such as the resurrection of Christ, His bodily ascension into heaven, etc. Anyone who holds the office of a prophet in your life and organization should adhere to this set of beliefs.

Many churches' core values are articulated in their statement of faith or mission statement. Make sure you are aware of the core values of the person whom you are considering appointing. Some beliefs are nonnegotiable, but there can be others that are supplemental beliefs that are not core. For example, some people who serve on my prophetic team have radically different eschatological beliefs than me. We agree to disagree on these types of values because they do not violate our core beliefs.

If you have any areas in which you disagree, it's okay; talk it through. Disagreement is healthy in normal relationships. As long as we all agree that Jesus is coming back to get His reward, then I am fine with them clearly being wrong (just kidding). But I am fine with them having their own convictions here. I do ask that while they are serving on our teams or directly inside our ministry, they agree not to teach on their version of eschatology. This has never caused us a problem.

Ultimately, there is work in appointing prophetic people. You are partially responsible for the administration of their gift from that point on. I would encourage you to set up a system with the person where you can weigh and test their words, but put the responsibility on them.

We ask all of our team members to track their own prophetic words. If they provide any trackable information, such as dates or coming future events, then they write down the person's name and email address and follow up within a given period of time. If our team members' prophetic words are wrong or even slightly off, then they take responsibility. When we have our check-in times as a team, we go over some of these things together in a non-judgmental way. It's a time where we can all grow.

Following the model Christ set with His disciples, we want to create a spiritual culture based on clear biblical core values. By doing so, we provide the necessary weights and measures by which a developing prophetic person can grow. In the safety of such a spiritual culture, you will provide increasing support and healthy structures to maintain what is working.

DEFINING PROPHETIC RESPONSIBILITIES

In the Old Testament, prophets provided governing words. Their responsibility came from the prophetic word itself. The structure they needed in order to thrive came from the words they were giving.

In the New Testament, we already have the structure in place for the operation of this office: Christ is the structure, and the Holy Spirit is our helper. The responsibly of the words given is already biblically constructed.

THE ADMINISTRATIVE DUTIES OF A PROPHET

Let's look at 1 Corinthians 14:29-33, where Paul talks about prophetic structure, particularly when it comes to administration:

> *Let two or three prophets speak, and let the others pass judgment. But if a revelation is*

*made to another who is seated, the first one
must keep silent. For you can all prophesy one
by one, so that all may learn and all may be
exhorted; and the spirits of prophets are subject
to prophets; for God is not a God of confusion
but of peace, as in all the churches of the saints.*

Appointed by Jesus Christ, the lead prophet has a self-governing responsibility. The spirit of the prophet is subject to the prophet. There is a divine structure that the prophet is called to. It is not who speaks in what turn. It is about the facilitation of the gift and office in a way that provides soundness and completeness in hearing and delivery. The prophets have self- and group accountability.

The prophet has a responsibility to administer his or her gifts in an orderly fashion. The prophet also facilitates and helps oversee the church and the direction in which it is going. He hears the heart of God and expresses how he feels. He helps prepare God's people for trials and tribulations on a grand scale.

When there is sin in the church, and nothing is being done about it, this prophet is the one to expose it. He is compelled to call for repentance and restoration, and in the worst case, remove such people (see Jeremiah 1:9-10). When I think of the administration-related duties of the prophet, I think of the major prophets of Israel who were committed to God's will in the face of adversity from their own kinsmen.

The responsibilities of a prophet regarding administration are:

- To connect to God in deep relationship and through this to hear from God for the people to whom they are appointed;

- To help train and teach or activate people to hear from God;

- To help others understand the revelation that God is giving them; and

- To help bring interpretation and application to prophetic words that have come to the people they are assigned to.

Prophets are proactive in their actions, not reactive. This intentionality is born out of their years of walking closely with the Father and fine-tuning their spiritual ear to hear His voice.

Their recognition as a leader among prophets brings with it greater responsibility. To be seated in the role of prophet is more than a title of honor; it is a calling born out of years of experience, trial and error, and of practicing the prophetic in all its forms.

APPOINTMENT TO THE OFFICE OF A PROPHET

We have studied how these gifts of Christ, the offices of prophet, are still prevalent and available today. We now want to discuss how to govern these offices and how to appoint people correctly. We went over the theological foundation of a prophet, including what they are and what they do, but now we need to look at a model for appointing them.

What are we appointing them to do? What responsibilities do they have? What type of accountability should we place around them?

The following responsibilities should be considered and goals should be set around these criteria (for those items that apply to your church or ministry):

1. A prophet helps the community they serve understand the times and seasons they are in. Sometimes they do this by giving prophetic messages to the leadership, congregation, or members.

2. A prophet helps team members process their revelation (not just revelation given through the prophet, but revelation given by team members and of corporate words as well).

3. A prophet helps equip people in their growth process of hearing God for themselves. They help set the context of faith for hearing God. They do this through teaching, prayer and impartation, modeling publicly and privately, mentoring, etc.

4. A prophet helps to discern and remove spiritual stumbling blocks from the community. They help see distractions or potential areas of spiritual warfare.

5. A prophet regularly prophesies over the movement they are involved with.

Now that we have defined the responsibilities of a prophet, let's look at a checklist of attributes and qualifications for appointing a prophet.

1. Do you have relationship with them? Have they just blown onto the scene, or do you know their history and track record? Also, how much time have you spent with them? Remember, relationship is vital.

2. How long have you been tracking them and their words? Can you recognize at least ten of their corporate words for others or for your ministry as having come to pass in a recent time period? Have any of their prophecies about your history been definers or helper words to bring strategy or definitive moments about who you are? How about their individual words: Have they helped people in your ministry move forward in their destiny and purpose?

3. Have you watched them prophesy in person? Witness their gift firsthand by having them practice on people you trust. Lay out the starter plan for them, letting them know how you expect them to serve. Then communicate the plan to the community or leaders whom they will help serve in their prophetic capacity.

    I always encourage leaders to make one-year and five-year plans that they can share with the rest of the team. This clarifies expectations both ways and gives everyone a clear vision of the role the prophet is playing. They know what they are doing and don't have expectations for things that they never agreed to or that you are not appointing.

4. If they minister outside your organization, or if your organization is multi-locational, then do your due diligence and check their past words

and how they came to pass. Check with their other references. It's like my cowboy barber used to say: "I can always take it off. I just can't put it back on." In other words, work with them on character issues, tracking responsibilities, self-governance, counseling, and inner healing *before* you appoint them—rather than after.

5. Set healthy expectations for their comings and goings. Just as in a local church, if you don't set expectations for their role (as you do for a worship leader or volunteer usher), then they will define their role for you. They might otherwise come only when they want to or work too often and burn themselves out.

   Because many organizations don't define the role well, prophetic people receive some entitlement on what they want to do. This can cause them to stop serving in other capacities that are helpful to the community. Prophets don't have the permission to do whatever they want; they should be invited into a healthy structure that provides them with context.

6. Make sure they have been nurtured in their gift with the best biblical core values. One of the things that I establish in *Translating God* is how Paul never wrote up specific character requirements for prophets. Why? Because he clearly shared character requirements for all believers, which applied completely to those who would fit into the category of prophets. The same burden to love, build character, be a servant, and more, applies fully to their growth.

   Remember that God is no respecter of persons (see Acts 10:34); He loves the volunteer usher as much as the most gifted prophet. Unfortunately, however, I have known some leaders who were so enamored with the prophet in their midst that they tended to brush off bad behavior and character issues. This is extremely detrimental to your community and contrary to the core value of relationship based on impartiality and trust.

7. Commit to a relational journey with the person and define times when you will connect with them. Get this into both of your calendars so that it's a hard date. Don't appoint someone to this role with whom you won't be willing to connect at least four times a year (once a quarter).

    When a prophetic person is out of sight, they might also be out of mind, and you will stop getting the benefit of their gift. Or if there is new direction you need to steer them in, it might be hard if they have been left alone or are comfortable in what they are doing.

    Also, meeting regularly face to face gives you a chance to notice the propensities of your prophet. They might have some great areas of focus like the arts, poverty, or leadership development, and you can begin to help steer their gift in those areas.

    Or they may have some negative propensities, such as harping on about sin or overusing mystical words that are hard for the average person to understand. As leaders immersed in prophetic language on a daily basis, we sometimes forget that the average—or casual—church attender may not actually know what the Leviathan spirit is! (I'm only half joking.)

8. Make sure you maintain a relationship with them in which you can speak into their process as it pertains to your organization. They should be open to this feedback.

As we nurture others in their prophetic journey, remember that, ultimately, you are not in control—God is. These are not *your* prophets or prophetic brothers and sisters. They have callings that are unique from yours and your team. The challenge is to build those bridges of relational trust so that iron may truly sharpen iron and so that the gift of prophecy is exercised in all its biblical beauty and bounty.

15 | APPOINTING A PROPHET FOR AN ORGANIZATION

When you appoint someone to the office of prophet in your organization, you are publicly recognizing them for their gift, character, and fruit. What expectations should you develop around them within your church or ministry?

Although I could give you several starter models, I don't want to provide cookie-cutter scenarios that simply can't fit every situation or organization. That's because each ministry, marketplace company, entertainment group, and politician has different needs for the prophetic. Like a Venn diagram, some of the roles and responsibilities will overlap, but others will not. But let me start a conversation with you.

It is more than okay to set some expectations for anyone in a service role to you—whether it's for employees who work in your company, a counselor whom you see once a week, or a teacher whose class you take. Clearly set expectations are normal in every other role that people take in our lives, so why can't we set expectations for prophets? It is actually unproductive and unhealthy not too.

HOW TO COMPENSATE IN THE PROPHETIC

As the Church begins to better value the prophetic, we will start to put budget and resources toward building it. Prophetic ministers and prophets have the catalytic ability to release others into prophetic ministry and to help them understand what God is already showing them. We need these people empowered in those roles because when they are, the water level goes up for us all.

If a person is working, they are worth the honor, recognition, finances, and opportunity commensurate with their service. They should be recognized and compensated fairly, even someone in a prophetic role. To take time and energy from someone for your own use or the use of your vision, without compensating them, is usury. In other words, we need to establish good boundaries.

Opportunity is a great motivator, but it can't be the permanent compensation. As a person gains more and more expertise in their ministry, they are going to have to be awarded compensation differently.

When someone is serving in a prophetic role, we have to determine their value to our organization. This can take time, especially if it's our first time inviting this role into the ongoing foundation of our staff.

Here is a scale of compensation according to expertise and value added for the prophetic:

1. THE OPPORTUNITY ITSELF. Sometimes just giving someone opportunity is enough, and financial compensation is not needed. Examples might

include a volunteer leader with a missional calling to support your organization, or someone new to the prophetic. In these cases, the opportunity itself can be compensation enough, particularly for a specified season. You can come to an agreement in which the prophet takes a volunteer role, but in that case, it really only works when there is minimal responsibility.

2. RECOGNITION AND HONOR. When you appoint and recognize a prophet into leadership, you are showing that you greatly value their position. Most of the time, those who grow into their gift as a prophet do it in a volunteer role. So, by recognizing and honoring their gift, it increases the impact of their place in your ministry. Not only is it a great motivator, but also it establishes a climate of expectation in the people who will be impacted by the prophet's ministry. By officially recognizing their role as a prophet within your ministry, it also gives them outside opportunities and establishes their credibility with other organizations and churches.

3. FOR CHURCH/MINISTRY ORGANIZATIONS. Set up a department and give them a budget. Maybe it's not yet time to pay your prophetic team or advisors, but they are doing enough where they just need space or finances to build. My main prophetic team leader builds our team around dinners and meetings where they get together socially. I have invested money and food over the years to help value what they are doing.

It could be that they need an office in your church (perhaps after hours, if you have limited space) to practice, train, or take ministry appointments. Or perhaps you could encourage them to build an entire service around the prophetic and help them establish it by giving them space and resources. Some of your more mature prophets could even host paid workshops or seminars once or twice a year to help underwrite their departmental budget.

4. FINANCES. When we talk about paying a person as a prophetic advisor or to be the prophetic team member on deck, there are many ways to do it. If you are their primary or only organization and you want to acknowledge and build the prophetic ministry or gift in your midst, then you can pay them to teach classes, nurture groups, and train ministry. If you are in a workplace or marketplace field, then you can pay them as an advisor, much like you would pay a business coach or success advisor. If they are going to serve in an ongoing capacity, then come up with a stipend, salary, or hourly rate and put some actual structure to their role.

I have seen people who were raised up as prophets who were never valued financially, and so there was a lack of long-term connection to the role. Either their role as prophet-in-residence wasn't defined well or it faded in its definition. When you get actual finances involved, both you and the prophet will take their role more seriously because you have put value to it.

Where your treasure is, there is your heart (see Matthew 6:21). This is so true, even in ministry roles such as a prophet.

AUTHORITY STRUCTURE

Make sure to define how the authority structure works in your organization and church and where your newly appointed prophet or prophetic ministry fits. Build their role into your organizational flow chart. Who will do their annual review? Determine their direct reports and let everyone they interface with know.

What is the conflict-resolution process, and how will you handle any negative reports between them and those with whom they are in relationship? In other words, what if someone has a bad experience with them one on one and you have to supervise the situation on a leadership level? Who will talk with them, who will help resolve the conflict, and who is the person to whom they will report?

By clarifying these processes and authority issues, you will be reducing potential future conflicts. Also, if someone does not have authority over the prophet, then they should not speak over them or into their process. Keep those lines of authority clear and clean.

RELATIONAL EXPECTATIONS

One of the most important things to do as you appoint a prophet is to put some relational requirements in place. If you don't do it on the front end, then you will regret it in the long term, because course correction gets a lot more difficult with time.

The prophet should also be more than okay with an open-door policy when it comes to relational connection. In particular, they need to be readily available for whomever they are interfacing with. If not, they are not the right person to be working with.

SET SOME PROPHETIC GOALS TOGETHER

Set some goals for your organization. Ask the prophet to prayerfully consider your church or company and provide any thoughts on a regular basis. This would be good to schedule when you are both available. We have a prophetic intercessor for our company who gives us a report that we go over prayerfully once a month. While it is always a good report for us to look at, every few months it becomes a definitive tool that is very helpful to us!

NON-LEADING PARTICIPATION

Ask your prophet to participate in your local or annual events. If you are a local church and you have a local prophet or prophetic team, then they should be attending the majority of your services. Think about it in the context of how many times an associate pastor, children's pastor, worship leader, or volunteer coordinator has to be plugged in for their role to bear fruit.

It is the same for a prophetic person; their role is just not always as visible to the rest of the church. If you run a company, include them in corporate parties, board meetings (or board-meeting dinners if there is sensitive information), vision-casting sessions, etc. If you are an apostolic movement, then have them come to your key gatherings during the year. Have the prophet visit any of your key leaders, team meetings, or families at least once every few years to build rapport but also to get their eyes on your world.

LEADING PARTICIPATION

If you believe it is time to have them participate actively in leadership, then set their expectations for their specific roles and tasks. I mentioned earlier about setting one-year and five-year goals and plans. Also, set up a structure in which they can feed your organization. One of the best ways the people of God profited from a prophet in the Bible was through schools or teaching, and this fits well within many organizations (see 1 Samuel 19:18-24; 2 Kings 2; 4:38-44).

If you are hiring them as a consultant for your company or ministry (rather than as staff), you will need to be more purposeful about building touch points between them and your executives and team leaders. Get them on the calendar to connect spiritually with your key people on a regular basis. Whatever it is you are asking them to do, schedule it on a calendar and set goals that you can both agree too.

PROVIDE AN ATMOSPHERE FOR THEM TO GROW

The prophetic is a relational tool set and prophets are relational creatures who grow in a nurturing environment. God Himself desires us to grow and build as a team. If they are part of your local church or movement, then figure out how to invest in their spiritual growth.

I love how one of the church movements I was invested in paid for all their prophetic people to attend a prophetic conference once a year. At least once a year, they were able to further develop their skill, exposure, and perspective. It could be that you send them to one of the prophetic gatherings around the world, pay for online theology classes, help them connect to a mentor for their growth, etc.

PROVIDE HONOR

Because the prophetic goes so undefined in so many movements and churches, there's very little direct honor given to them. Think about it: some of the prophets in modern history have helped avert world wars, changed the identity of corporations so that they could be successful, and given prophecies that have birthed church movements and denominations. But these stories are rarely told, even by the very denominations they helped start.

We touched on it earlier, but it's such an important facet of relational prophecy: We have to bring honor to the prophets we appoint. Recognize their gift and calling in a public way. Build a structure they can thrive in. Tell their God stories, because their stories are your story.

I am not trying to build just a "words of affirmation" culture, but I *am* encouraging you to look seriously at the issue of honor. How are the prophets or prophetic people in your midst perceived, received, and positioned in your world? It is your responsibility to help develop this structure, and it is their responsibility to thrive in it.

HAVE FAITH IN THEIR GIFTS

Another way to say this is to place a demand on the gift of God in them. Give them the opportunity to bloom by giving them assignments and projects. If they don't per-form in one area, don't let that be the last time you ask. Keep asking them to pray into situations, have them meet with you about areas you are trying to build, and ask them to seek God for you.

I asked my team to pray about a conference I wanted to put on and no one received any revelation about it. Then after we hosted the first one, I had many prophetic words about doing a second one. I wasn't even planning to have a part two or a series, but that is what happened. It started with me opening up the opportunity to include God in my decisions and then leaning into people He talks to. Some of the words provided very creative insight into how to brand and position our meetings—ideas I never would have thought of.

THEOLOGY OF THE PROPHET

Theology is so critical because whatever theology a prophet embraces will determine the bent or slant of their words. Getting to know their theology might take time, but you need to make sure they are in sync when it comes to your statement of faith, leadership beliefs, and basic core theological values.

Many people have an amazing prophetic anointing but a theological foundation that is less than solid. This can be detrimental if you actually bring them into the core of what you are building as a prophetic ministry.

DEVELOP THEIR ROLE OVER TIME

When prophetic ministry roles are undeveloped in a movement or church, a common mistake is to give a prophet too many rights and entitlements upfront. There should be progressive growth and a model of what they are growing into, even if you have never corporately accessed that level of the prophetic before. This way, as they progress in faithfulness to God and in using their life and gifts to assist you, you can progressively allow them access to your world of influence.

There are many ways to manage their progression. Perhaps it's an issue of who they have access to minister to, how much public time they get if you have a public side to ministry, what meetings they get invited to, etc.

Think of it the same way you would, say, a potential worship leader who begins in a support role. In that case, in order to successfully bring them on board, you will need to build what that role means in relationship to the current team. You will need to give them space to build credibility as leaders with the congregation and lean heavily into their talent, skill, and gifting to lead worship.

Ultimately, you are going to have to provide them with a process that builds faith and credibility. Otherwise, if you just suddenly place them onstage alongside a worship team that already has loyalty with your congregation, then you are setting them up for a rocky road.

Maybe they co-lead every other week, go to all the worship practices, sing songs that the church already knows, and introduce new songs less frequently for a while as they build rapport and authority. Each process might be a little different depending on the skill, experience, gifting, relational maturity, character, and anointing of the person you are bringing on.

Bringing a prophet into your ministry environment is very similar. You need a process based on their connection to you and your church, their level of gifting, and their maturity. If they have an established ministry and are coming in to partner with you, the access to your church might be much different than if you are raising someone up.

Also, their level of gifting and impact in the community will slow or speed things up as some people just are more connected or gifted than others. We want to honor relationship but also gifting. If you are raising them up for a specific role of operating in the prophetic, then it's okay to weigh and measure both.

I have seen imbalance on both sides: a prophet who may violate relational culture but who is prophetically gifted, and those who honor the culture but are not highly gifted prophetically. The worst is to see a prophetic person who is both relational and gifted be overlooked for someone who is out of balance.

My current prophetic team leader, Lorri, started as my assistant leader and then became my co-leader. I built the department by making every decision with her, then after co-teaching five classes and a lot of leading and experience, she took over. She brings in new prophetic team members, leads our team meetings before our events, and does the debriefing in the team meetings after. The point is that Lorri grew into the full role she now serves in.

Years ago, I was brought into a church in Kansas City called Metro Christian Fellowship as a prophetic minister. I was brought into a monthly general staff meeting to hear what was happening, to connect relationally, but also to pray for revelation. Also, I sent in a monthly report to share what God was showing me in the prophetic realm.

I did a lot of ministry of a wide variety for the church, but it was a few years before they gave me a platform at conferences or services.

At one point the senior leader defined the requirements for public prophetic ministry and service, and some
of us felt called to that. So, as we kept serving faithfully,
a group of us met those requirements and were afforded
the freedom to take a microphone during worship or ministry times in pretty much any meeting.

We were wanted because we were bearing good fruit;
and because we were bearing fruit, we were given free
public reign. The reports from what happened with the
few of us who were designated seemed to always be
of great benefit to those we were ministering to. It was
humbling and amazing to be trusted with the freedom
and prophetic appointment we were given.

If releasing prophetic people is new to you, take the
advice of Proverbs 15:22: "Plans fail for lack of counsel,
but with many advisers they succeed." Invite trusted
ministry friends, advisors, elders, and board members
into the conversation for some solid feedback. Consider
their thoughts, as they should be looking out for your best
interests. Define the big picture of what a prophet could
look like in your organization, then determine what level
you want them to enter into with you. Their appointment
can grow as their fruits grow.

God will continue to show favor on them, so you should
also. Bring to mind the benefits they have brought forth in
your organization and place them in a position that is best
suited for you and their callings. If they are a prophetic
teacher, allow them the chance to teach in groups, and
then in your leadership, and eventually publicly.

As your leaders and small groups respond to their role,
life and gift, you will see if they are suitable to teach the
new and old. Make sure to start off with a solid foundation of growth and expectation.

Why would you go through all the trouble to grow someone within your organization and appoint them? Because it is God's design for a perfect church, and you will see the blessing of God when His church structure is operating this way.

16 | BECOMING A PROPHET IN AN ORGANIZATION

What if we could proactively pursue the prophetic gifts through someone we respect and honor by asking them to volunteer or by paying them as a prophetic advisor? You might be a church making room for this role, or a businessperson looking for someone to help carry the spiritual culture of your workplace in their heart, or maybe a politician who needs regular eyes on their career or jurisdiction.

What opportunities would this afford us, as the Church, if we knew how to activate the prophetic and invite prophetic ministry people into our world? Or even to partner with a prophet in our business, creative pursuit, or career?

PROPHETIC ADVISORS

Just as most companies, churches, and political groups have a board, why not actually put together a prophetic advisory board to pray into decisions that are being

269

made? If the prophetic was one of the most powerful roles in the Bible, how do we set expectations for how to honor it in this day and age? And not to just *wish* or *hope* it will happen, but to set ourselves up for the expected opportunity?

I took my first volunteer role as a prophetic advisor for a business in the 1990s. They asked me to regularly meet with the team and pray for them, as well as whenever they were making intense decisions. I was on call for them about once a month. It was an exciting partnership because the CEO was really trying to have a kingdom-culture business where families were prioritized and his employees felt like their spiritual purpose was as important as their natural purpose.

In the beginning, most of the employees were Christians from our church community, and it was very much a mom and pop shop. God had a bigger dream for this group, though, and over a two-year period they went through explosive growth. Along with the success came a lot of spiritual upheaval and even some very real problems they had to wrestle with. It was the best of times and the worst of times.

I played a role as coach, counselor, advisor, and friend, which are all functions attributed to the Holy Spirit, and also what modern prophetic ministry should feel like. More often than not, I brought spiritual perspective that I released through conversations more than through direct prophetic words. But over those two years, I was privileged to play a part in shaping the company and also helping them to avert some real crises in their workforce.

Eventually I had to transition out because of the time it was taking up. I just wasn't readily available, so we installed a new person. They had my successor pray with prophetic expectation once a week and give an email or phone message once a month. They also included her in board meetings every six months to listen and pray.

Afterward, they would meet and she would share—sometimes prophetically—what she was hearing from God. She had such a radical impact on the growth and health of the company that after two years they hired her in her role. All these years later she is still there, serving as a prophetic minister in the marketplace.

If you have been appointed as a prophet or prophetic minister to an organization, what is next? Let's look at some of the possible roles you can play.

PRAYER AND INTERCESSION

It is time to ponder in your heart the people God has assigned to you. Setting aside time to pray into their journey is so important. You can do this practically in a scheduled time, but each one of you will do it differently. Some of my team spends time with God in the mornings on walks, while others are night owls. Some spend hours in intercession, while others spend fifteen minutes to find the same place of connection with God.

I have appointments set on my phone to pray for different people with whom I have an assignment, and I try to pray for an hour or so for all of them. Sometimes this looks like listening prayer; sometimes I reread past words I gave, pondering their current state, or imagining their future with God. Each of us has a different process, but one thing is for certain: If you don't schedule the time to pray, you probably won't be faithful to spend it.

KNOW YOUR ASSIGNMENT: RESEARCH AND STUDY

Get to know the organization, church, or movement you are being brought into. Spend time if you can with the leadership upfront. Also get to know what they are building in terms of vision, mission, and strategy. Some of this can be simple, like looking through their website, public materials, bios, etc.

Some people are afraid that the more they know, the less useful they will be. But actually, the more you relationally connect to the people, the more your heart will be a landing strip for God. Plus, when you see what kinds of activities, staff, events, mission statement, and culture they have, you will really begin to personalize your assignment and adopt them into your heart.

I believe Daniel had this type of firsthand opportunity to understand Babylon's people, politics, and culture, and yet it didn't limit him at all from prophesying when it was time. It actually kept him connected to the Babylonians instead of just remaining Hebrew-centric.

Daniel's experience is in stark contrast to Jonah, who only knew the sin of the Ninevites so was incredibly offended when they repented. Jonah saw no redemptive value in them because he didn't see them as lovable. In short, his heart was not connected to his assignment.

Jonah just wanted justice from heaven. He had to go on an inward journey (both literally and figuratively) to experience a heart change. He had to change so that he could steward the love of God and the mercy of His heart for a people group that were undeserving.

I know prophets who don't like to receive any upfront information about a person or organization before they prophesy, and I understand that. But I have never been limited by information that I knew beforehand when I prophesied. At times I have had to qualify that I know some things first though.

REPORTING YOUR REVELATION

Whether they set your expectation for how often you are going to report or you set theirs, it's important to have regular connecting time on what God is showing you. Reporting patterns can vary radically. For instance, I'm involved with a once-a-year roundtable experience where we share and someone takes notes. I spend several times during the year putting together what God is showing me and present it there.

Another group I am in relationship with likes to receive a monthly report, which I provide in the form of a one- to three-page bullet-point report. Every few months we touch base by phone to follow up on the last few reports. Yet another group is way more organic, and I just share with them whenever the revelation comes or whenever we have time together.

My favorite people to serve are those who value and respect what the prophetic can do. Everyone has their own culture and style, but I do appreciate the journeys in which we touch base monthly or quarterly through reporting. Regular interaction and dialogue are what build, reinforce, and activate prophetic expectation!

PROCESSING THE SPIRITUAL JOURNEY OF REVELATION

One of the most important things you can do for an organization is to help them process their journey of revelation. The main group with whom I am a prophet meets with me once a year. We review significant words they have received, share the spiritual or prophetic history that year, and then pray together. My role is to help them navigate through their major prophetic words and actions.

I try to bring validation to the key points and also help recognize blind spots with them or for them. Having someone to process the spiritual and revelatory parts of the journey is so key for a business owner, apostle, church leader, musician, etc.

HELPING TO ACTIVATE OTHERS IN REVELATION

One thing I already talked about that I learned from Bob Jones is to really listen to other people's dreams, encounters, words, and prophesies. Nothing activates faith quite like when someone who is respected validates your experience. Think about a reality TV show like *The Voice* (or whatever iteration of that show you might have in your country—*The Voice UK*, etc.). One of the most powerful moments on this singing competition show is when world-class musicians tell the contestants that they hear superstardom in their voice.

You can just see the contestant's heart and imagination grow ten times its size in that moment! When you help someone navigate what God is showing them and validate it as real, you are equipping them to go after more.

It is also good to learn how to teach or mentor the prophetic gifts in a one-on-one structure. Although this won't be every prophet's function, the majority can give a basic prophetic activation or mentoring session in one sitting. People thrive under one-on-one tutoring or instruction. And sometimes, everything they have learned from seminars, conferences, and books comes together through that relational connecting time of a one-on-one experience.

Some of you will also become teachers of the prophetic in your local group, ministry, church, or beyond. We need prophetic trainers! If this is a passion for you, there is plenty of room to help activate people! Start in the micro and God can raise you up to the macro.

HELPING TO DISCERN: BECOMING A WATCHMAN

Many prophets find themselves in a role of discerning what needs to move forward in lives, ministries, and businesses—especially in interpersonal relationships. A lot of prophetic people can even discern or see what the enemy is trying to do, whether or not there is warfare, and the specifics if there is spiritual attack. When this happens, and the prophetic voice is added to the spiritual arsenal to combat the enemy, the prophet helps become part of the solution to see what God is doing.

Discernment in the area of spiritual warfare is such a valuable role, but sometimes I think the emphasis can be overplayed. It is easiest to see what the enemy is doing or to fixate on man's weakness, but it takes a strong anointing to focus on what God is doing and to help usher that into a situation.

I am going to make a broad generalization: Typically when I consult a church about prophets they have appointed, and especially when I meet a marketplace team that has used one, almost always the prophet is focused on the strategy of the enemy or on warfare. I love the watchman role, I feel I play it well, but it is a role of focus on *who God is* and what *He* is doing. It shouldn't feel like the enemy is the main player. God should be front and center.

As you lead people in your prophetic role, make sure they have more solutions than problems, that they have more God focus than enemy focus, that they have more strategy of God than strategy of the enemy. Undoubtedly, negative discernment gets more attention than positive revelation until you personally mature; then the positives begin to build more than the negatives tear down.

We were made to build even more than to war.

The war is already won and will eventually fade away, but the building of God's will and nature never ceases.

BUILDING RELATIONAL ACCOUNTABILITY

Learning how to submit to relational and spiritual authority can be a difficult thing.

If you are under authority with your pastor, he could be responsible for helping with your spiritual welfare. If it's an apostle, he might be responsible for your ministry health as well. If you run your own ministry, perhaps your covering authority is a mature group of believers who make up your board.

You have to set yourself up to be accountable for positive reasons, but also when negative things happen.

FOR PROPHETIC MINISTERS OR A LOCAL CHURCH PROPHET: It is good to have a local pastor and a few strong ministry friends who serve as an advisory team. We are talking about people who really know you and know each other. Your church might help set this up or provide this as a covering for your service of being released in ministry with them.

This is good to define because these are people you would trust if you go through a controversy, or people who would help speak into your character if you hit conflict with someone. Also, it is important for people to be able to pursue the biblical model of conflict resolution with you that is laid out in Matthew 18.

If they have an issue with you and they are connected to what you are doing, they should be able to talk to you about it. If that doesn't satisfy them, they should be able to seek a mediator in your accountability circle, like your pastor or one of the other appointed leaders in your life. This is important because prophecy is both a relational and a power gift, so people need to be able to share concerns at times with you.

Getting these lines of authority in place clearly and strongly can help you avoid unnecessary conflicts. For example, if your pastoral covering also appoints the prophetic in their ministry or church, and controversy arises with another prophetic person, you don't want to find yourself in the middle of it—especially if you didn't do anything wrong. By clarifying your role and your authority figures' expectation of theirs, you can avoid being penalized—or your role minimized—by your authority structure or becoming collateral damage in another person's controversy.

FOR PROPHETS: It is good to have an apostolic leader in your life as part of your covering or accountability. Also, it is good for you to have your own organization. In America you might want to become a 501(c)3, or nonprofit, which has its own governing board. These board members should have an apostolic bent or wisdom in the ministry sphere, especially if they are businesspeople.

These are the people who are going to help you if something happens where there is a conflict, international dispute, aggressive campaign against you, etc. If your only authority covering is your local pastor or a single apostle, they probably won't have the ability to slow down enough to handle your crisis with full attention (through no fault of their own).

I am certainly not saying a pastor couldn't walk with you through the crisis; I am saying that if you also have a team, then there is greater capacity to help you handle a crisis. These can be two separate groups of people: your pastor, who is your frontline, day-to-day authority, and a board or advisory team, there on more of a quarterly or annual basis, but super-efficient in a crisis.

Imagine that you have the right accountability and board structure and someone accuses you of sexual harassment, cheating in prophetic words, manipulation, or bad theology. You want people who can actually walk with you through the whole process. Or if there is something more down to earth going on, such as marriage problems, a rebellious child, or a financial crisis, you also want an accountability structure that can take the time to bring advice, clarity, and direction.

I have also discovered a principle that is important for the favor and breakthrough that you bring: your apostolic leader will know how to help you to tell these stories and track with you in a way that a local pastor who is not apostolic won't always connect to in the same way.

An apostle has a building gift to see the big picture that is beyond just a local church. And when you are a prophet, you are typically called beyond just one local congregation. You might be called to an industry, a nation, or another macro sphere of influence. In this case, you need to track with someone apostolic who can help cover you and see you there.

Here are a few more reasons to seek accountability:

- The people you are accountable to help establish your credibility.
- They will help you not be alone in controversy but will walk with you.
- They will fight for you when people persecute you.
- They will cheer you on when you hit milestones of growth.
- They will support you when there are spiritual ebbs and lulls to your flows.
- They will remind you of the days you were most in tune or anointed by God and will keep your stories in front of you.

The following are what accountability provides when hard things happen:

- When someone attacks your credibility, your long-term accountability will help you because you will have people standing with you.
- If someone accuses you of lying or cheating, you will have character witnesses.
- If someone dissects your word theologically, you have a mature team to help you walk through the process.

- If someone drags your name or reputation through the mud, you have someone to fight with you or to mediate on your behalf.
- They will help you to have faith, even when people are coming against you.

FRUITFULNESS AS A CENTRAL QUALIFIER

In order to appoint someone into the office of a prophet, consider the qualifiers of a prophet and the fruit of their life, both relationally and in ministry. Do they produce prophetic words that bring actual change, advancement, connection to resources and opportunities, miracles and signs and wonders? Is there substance?

Do they help your ministry, movement, or organization navigate the revelation that God is giving you? Do they have God's gifts at work in their life? Do they live a life of integrity and of good character?

Measure their first fruitfulness in life just as Paul instructed Timothy to do toward elders in 1 Timothy 3. Measure their fruitfulness in ministry as the apostles did before they commissioned prophets and apostles and sent them out.

Believe it or not, there are many people who become good at prophetic language, claim to have a lot of encounters, but have no tangible fruit in their life as a result of their perceived prophetic role. This should be taken seriously and weighed when you are looking to appoint someone. Can you list 10 to 20 times that you or the people close to you have seen firsthand words that manifested something?

I was brought into an international church-planting ministry recently to evaluate with them the prophets they had appointed. I was helping them rethink their structure and roles. There were many defined prophets, and I asked a question regarding what they were trying to establish in the role of the prophetic within their movement.

We then went around the table to each person who had been appointed, and we realized together that many were not fulfilling the purpose of their intended role. What the ministry had intended to build in them was either not being served or not being fulfilled.

The problem was that this movement had been around for a long time, and some of the prophets had the perception that they had the equivalent of "tenure" in the ministry. They were in their role for life because of the price they had paid. We had a problem: some were no longer functioning as prophets in the ministry.

They taught some and they spent time with people, but the fruit of the prophetic wasn't evident anymore. The role this movement felt they were supposed to play biblically was not happening through the people they had appointed.

It took *a lot* of course correction because they had never created a plan, structure or expectation for the prophetic. The activity of the prophetic had run its course and now, decades later, they were no longer parallel in their goals as compared to the movement by which they were appointed. It was a painful reorganization, but the budget, energy, and position of prophet are now being built with people who want to grow them.

If you are in any growing organization, then you are experiencing growth in all roles, jobs, functions, budgets, gifts, and fruitfulness. Typically, when I have helped chart out the prophetic for movements and organizations, that is the one area that hasn't changed or grown within the organization. Or if the prophetic has been active, it's mostly reactive growth instead of powered growth that comes with purposeful planning and goal setting.

If we as a Church want to see God use the prophetic as a powerful evangelistic tool, then it needs to start with us—with a paradigm shift within our churches and ministries. As a leader you need to assess what you believe God wants to build prophetically in your ministry, church, or organization.

Goal setting, articulated expectations, boundaries, and clear job descriptions (or volunteer descriptions) have to apply to the prophetic just like any other role you are raising up. If successful, not only can you have the benefit of the gift, but also you can create a culture that provides an ability to host the presence of God through the prophetic.

17 | FATHERS AND MOTHERS

The apostle Paul wrote the architectural language for most of the New Testament. Most biblical scholars believe Paul wrote 13 books (of course when he penned them, they were written as letters). That's nearly *half* of the entire New Testament.

Paul spoke into prophecy on many occasions. As well, he said some vital things that can help us imitate his process for the prophetic, just as he instructed us to do.

There are two very important components that I extract from 1 Corinthians 4:14-16. First, prophets and prophetesses should have an accountability structure that provides a father- or mother-type relationship in their lives. This usually comes in the form of an apostolic leader and/or sometimes a more senior prophet. Second, Paul provides us with a relational model by which we can implement accountability.

I want to talk a bit about both of these important elements, starting with accountability.

PATRIARCHS AND MATRIARCHS OF ACCOUNTABILITY

The "father and mother" model is probably one of the most attacked parts of accountability because so many prophetic people have (or had) dysfunctional relationships with their parents. As well, many prophets have walked a journey of misunderstanding with church leaders who they would have considered a father or mother.

I would say I am asked by people to be their spiritual dad at every event, every day on email, in every ministry school I visit. This is precious, and the reality is that we can only have so many spiritual children in whom we have a direct investment.

The problem is that we often look for the most visible ministers or leaders to become our spiritual mother or father instead of looking for godly, mature, healthy people right where we live. Let me share with you my own model, which may or may not work for you. I have had to work hard in my life to keep this relevant and working.

I have three types of spiritual parents in my life:

1. My life mentors, who happen to be my actual parents. My parents mentored me in the spiritual elements of life, not just the natural (and I know this is rare).

2. A few of my board members have father or older brother qualities that I rely on. These mentors make the time and space that my apostolic leaders don't have to process my life, heart, and spiritual journey in detail and great length.

3. My apostolic father and mother. These are the two people I get to spend the least amount of time with but whom I really trust. I keep them filled in a few times a year on what is going on in my life. They know when I am in a time of success and breakthrough as I share some of those stories. If there is controversy or pain, I also share those stories.

   They know they have the right to look into my life, share their thoughts and heart, and speak into my process. I look to them for courage to take on certain missions where feedback is especially critical (e.g., sending teams to the porn convention to do prophetic outreach, going into strip clubs in red light districts, confronting a pastor about an affair who is extremely well known, etc.).

The Bible sets up the hierarchy of leadership as a spiritual family with fathers and mothers, brothers and sisters, and sons and daughters. We also see patriarchs and matriarchs who sometimes represent the leaders of families who are not always the oldest. But still, they carry the weight of leadership for the family unit.

One such example is Joseph, who was actually the youngest of Jacob's twelve sons. Another is David, who was plucked from obscurity as a fledgling teenager to answer the call of God.

The Bible consistently plants the idea of relational accountability and growth in the context of family. This isn't a corporate-structure relationship but an actual family relationship with family dynamics.

If you are a prophet, then I believe you will benefit best by having a spiritual mother or father to have a voice into your heart. This does not necessarily mean they are the age of a father or mother to you, but that they carry weight to be able to share authority in your spiritual journey and speak into it.

They actually might be a younger brother or sister in some areas of life, or they might be a son or daughter in others. But when it comes to the authority God has put on them in spiritual leadership in ministry, they carry the weight of a spiritual mother or father.

With someone who is a spiritual covering or parent, there is also a submissive process. This doesn't mean we blindly submit all areas of our lives to their approval or direction, but it does mean our spiritual health and well-being are something we share with them in a vulnerable process. We are open to their input, direction, and sometimes even their agenda. There is tremendous health that comes for someone in proper alignment with a spiritual father and mother in their life.

For example, you may have a spiritual parent over your ministry who's not very gifted in one area, such as finances. Just because they are your spiritual parent doesn't mean you are to be affected by something that isn't going well in their life or submitting to that area. Many people get confused when it comes to being under spiritual authority and apply spiritual authority to common areas of life.

Just like grown adult kids don't need parents to tell them which job to take or what car to buy, so too submitting to spiritual parents as an adult in the spirit doesn't necessarily mean you are asking for all other practical areas to be covered. You are your own covering for those elements of your life.

Unfortunately, the concept of spiritual parental authority has been widely abused and misunderstood at times within prophetic and apostolic communities.

I am a spiritual father and patriarch to many people on my prophetic team, in my ministry, in the church we planted, and also to church leaders through our apostolic network. In some of these relationships I serve as the primary spiritual father, while with others I have a patriarchal voice into their life and process but don't carry the daily or regular caregiving role.

With some I am like an older brother figure. Some people who look to me as a spiritual father are successful in areas I don't understand, so I would never try to speak into or parent those areas.

It matters how you set up your covering. Your covering does not set itself up but is a process of mutual submission, connection and relationship.

The second thing we can see in 1 Corinthians 4:14-16 is that the apostle Paul looked into their situation and provided them with a relational solution. Accountability is relationally motivated, and by it, one's propensities, weaknesses, and faults are exposed through vulnerability. In the context of healthy relationships, the exposure brings awareness, healing and proper vulnerability.

Finding people who are spiritually mature to help others in their calling in the prophetic is a challenge at times. But if you pursue it and establish it, there will be amazing benefit. This is true even if the person doesn't fully understand your gift but holds your heart well. These kinds of accountable relationships make vulnerability possible.

Through transparency, you are able to open yourself up to a father or mother who can cover you and demonstrate the desired giftings, grace, and callings that you desire to walk in. As a result, this process of vulnerability builds expectations in you and grace for your life, but it also helps people relate to you.

WHAT SPIRITUAL FATHERS AND MOTHERS ARE NOT

THERAPIST. If you are having an emotional, mental, or relational breakdown that isn't within the ministry, you of course should be vulnerable to your spiritual father or mother. Your process of healing and resolution, however, should be with a Christian therapist. Hire a therapist, and then keep the leader in the loop on how it is going.

LIFE COACH. Many people try to access leaders to be their life coach or self-help guru. They are looking for a process of development that really needs to be personally motivated—not managed by the ministry you are a part of. Do you need more skill, biblical knowledge, practicum? Take courses, go to seminars, do online studies. Don't put the pressure of your personal growth and development on the person you are accountable to.

FINANCIAL ADVISOR. I have seen many people try to get resources and financial advice from their spiritual authority. This just doesn't make sense most of the time, unless they *are* a financial advisor or coach.

WHAT FATHERS AND MOTHERS ARE MEANT TO BE

I would encourage you to lean on the fathers and mothers that God has placed—or will place—in your life. If you're an orphan in your own mind, then you will always be alone. Elijah felt like there was no one like him and that he was alone, and the Lord rebuked him. God shared with Elijah that there were so many other prophets, and he could have had His support (see 1 Kings 19:4-14).

So how should we view a spiritual mother and father? Here are some principles.

IMITATOR

Imitate those around you who are walking in the giftings, callings and abilities that you desire to walk in. God places so much emphasis on the testimony of Jesus that we too can be living epistles read by everyone who is hungry.

This can be controversial, but I fully believe in the principle of it and have done it for decades: Imitate the men and women of God whom you look up to. Follow them online. Go to their meetings, seminars, and conferences. Even the wise men traveled to see Jesus.

It's okay for you to get out of your comfort zone and connect to the ministry of people that God has anointed in your generation. Most of the prophets who made history sat under the covering—or at least the teaching—of other prophets for seasons of their lives.

I even remember imitating the styles of how other people prophesied. This process of study and imitation helped shape who I am now as I learned from so many amazing prophets. This exploratory journey of prophetic identity is so precious and meaningful; you want to be a sponge and absorb everything there is to absorb and build off the foundation of everyone who has already paid a price.

ANSWERABILITY

Are you answerable for your actions? Listen to what Paul said:

> Then after an interval of fourteen years I went up again to Jerusalem with Barnabas, taking Titus along also. It was because of a revelation that I went up; and I submitted to them the gospel which I preach among the Gentiles, but I did so in private to those who were of reputation, for fear that I might be running, or had run, in vain.
>
> —GALATIANS 2:1-2, *NASB*

The apostle Paul gave a full account of the doctrine he preached. He provided a responsibility for explaining his actions among his peers. Someone who is willing to open up to their peers and provide a full account of their actions is positioned for leadership.

I have seen some who get to a place where they don't feel relationally required to answer for their thoughts and actions. Sadly, they have removed themselves from the place of accountability and they are a risk.

Jesus called Himself the good shepherd who stays at the gate to keep us from bounding out (see John 10:1-18). When someone wanders outside the sheep gate, they become isolated and attacked by the wolves. Also, when you are above correction, you are above advancement. Even the apostle Paul, who wrote 13 books of the New Testament, displays answerability.

So should we.

Have you retained your teachability as you've grown as a Christian, particularly in the prophetic realm?

> *And he began to speak out boldly in the synagogue. But when Priscilla and Aquila heard him, they took him aside and explained to him the way of God more accurately.*

—ACTS 18:26

People who have reached some level of success within their career or ministry generally think of themselves as experts in that field. A popular study listed in *Christianity Today* showed that most pastors think of themselves as being in the top 10 percent of the best communicators in the world. That means that most ministers overrate their influence, knowledge, and input to the world around them.

I love how popular psychologist Stephen Strand studied expertise in our generation and made the statement, "When people believe they are the expert of a specific field, they actually stunt their ability to grow by up to 90%. They lose their teachability."

The people from whom you take prophetic life direction and application should be teachable. If they are not, then they will soon level off in their perspective and experience. God continues to expand His kingdom; we need to be teachable enough to see it and partner with it.

Here are some ways to tell if someone is teachable:

- They learn from new sources regularly. They don't just have their golden oldies preachers, but they add current people, music, and influencers to their life to be on a learner's journey.

- They are confrontable. Whether you tell them that a prophecy they gave you was just a bit off or you actually need to do some relational confrontation, they are confrontable. And they can be confronted without pulling a power trip based on their gifting, authority, or perspective.

- They are open to trying new things and hearing about new ways God is expressing Himself, without having a know-it-all attitude or saying, "I have seen that before." These reactions are based in insecurity because either the person hasn't actually experienced it or genuine pride crops up where they think they have experienced everything.

- They are open relationally to hear from others' experiences and grow from them. They aren't the relationally dominant one all the time but enjoy listening.

INTEGRITY

Since I know, O my God, that You try the heart and delight in uprightness, I, in the integrity of my heart, have willingly offered all these things; so now with joy I have seen Your people, who are present here, make their offerings willingly to You.

—1 CHRONICLES 29:17, *NASB*

After training thousands of people in the prophetic, I can say with full conviction that integrity is one of the main character traits that needs mentoring the most. The desire to be profound, coupled with social affirmation, leads many to exaggeration, performance issues, and even lying.

This shouldn't be completely shocking though; consider the fact that the first man and woman had to leave the garden because of lies. I believe that when you set the goals of the prophetic correctly on love and protecting and building relationships, problems with integrity get minimized.

Honesty and strong moral principles are attributes that the Bible shows God delighting in as you read about the different people He loves. He is a God of truth and righteousness. The interesting thing about the prophetic and prophets is that you cannot separate the gift from the person. They are so intertwined, just like the spirit, soul, and body.

If someone is not walking in integrity, then it will show in their prophecies. Prophecy is a relational gift and it operates best under healthy relationships. If there is dishonesty, lying, or cheating, then the information given won't be life transforming because it won't be connected to what God is doing. It may sound good in the moment, but it will not be life giving.

TRANSPARENCY

> *Therefore, laying aside falsehood, speak truth each one of you with his neighbor, for we are members of one another.*
>
> —EPHESIANS 4:25, *NASB*

We approached transparency a few different ways in this book. One way that we covered this topic was through qualifying your prophetic words. If you are giving a word and you have common knowledge about the person, then you should qualify your prophecy so that you are honest in your confession. You don't want to come off as if you know more than you do.

The other way we approach transparency is through vulnerability. Being vulnerable in your process will help the person you are ministering to relate to your humanity while still receiving from God through you.

As I was growing in the prophetic, vulnerability was rarely modeled by my contemporaries. They usually only shared the story that they had victory in but often would hide their true stories of pain, suffering, family issues, etc. We now have a lot of helpful psychology in the Church that just wasn't available in the 1990s and before.

I'm talking about things like the discovery of identity, God's ability to be seen in our weakness, and allowing our true selves to be seen instead of a stage self or performance self. Unfortunately, much of this is not seen everywhere, although it is globalizing fast—even in the Western Church.

When I fail in something, I have no problem sharing it because I learn from it. As we established earlier, prophets don't have to be infallible, because there is forgiveness and grace in the New Covenant.

Vulnerability for someone growing in the prophetic is the ability to admit you don't always get things right or that you don't have all the interpretation and answers for the revelation you are getting.

If you currently have a spiritual father or mother in your life, that is awesome! Press into that relationship and gain from it all that God wants you to receive. If you are still searching for a spiritual patriarch or matriarch, sometimes you don't have to search far and wide. It's kind of like Dorothy at the end of the *Wizard of Oz* when she realizes that what she has been looking for all along has been right there in front of her.

Maybe your birth father or mother is actually your spiritual parent. If not—and I know for a lot of people that is not the case—then perhaps a grandparent, uncle or aunt? Another great place to seek out a spiritual parent is in your local church.

Pray and ask God to reveal that person to you and be open to how He answers your prayer.

CONCLUSION

As you have read throughout the book hearing God's voice is the most empowering way to live life. He loves us so much that He wired us to hear and has given us the Bible to develop the character of our identity so that we can become containers of this great privilege of intimacy with Him.

I think of all the times I have heard from God that have formed my journey or all the prophetic words that I have taken through a process just like described in this book and have seen such different results in life because of hearing and obeying.

The prophetic gifts should be one of the most encouraging aspects about Christianity. The fact that we still have prophets today and that God can use them to intervene and bring a Spiritual result to our natural process is not only one of our great benefits of Christianity but its also one of the ways that God shows His love and the fact that He divinely guides us. We are truly His children.

I was thinking about some friends who are not Christians who hit a wall in their marriage. They did the emergency trauma therapy, the long term counseling, built the support network around them and it was so hard. They didn't have a real vision of each other or their marriage. They kept getting unhinged at the seams of their relationship even though they are amazing and ran after tools of health and eventually much changed and thank God they are still together. At the same time there was another couple who were Christians and followed all the same steps the first couple I mentioned did. But then in the midst of it they prayed together, they fought for spiritual perspective on their marriage, on each other, and on themselves. They heard God deeply about each other and came into conviction about what they were doing wrong themselves. It created so much more synergy and helped them in a way that truly shows that hearing God doesn't just encourage us it moves us forward. He resolves things with spiritual resolution that we may not be able to get through in the tools that humanity offers.

My wife, Cherie, and myself have been on such a journey of helping people to feel empowered in life. We aren't trying to take the super out of God's supernatural ability, the reality is His nature truly is super and other than. We want to demystify these gifts, ministries, and even the office while keeping His glorious supernatural personhood intact in our hearts because He simply is not like us. Learning how to hear from God and then appointing this process or administrating it in our real lives is so rewarding because we benefit from letting the God who has a plan, strategy, and love for us lead us. A lot of people in our modern self managed independent society don't want this kind of relationship with God because they compare it to controlling leadership or to weakness to be lead not just by our convictions but by the power and person of the Holy Spirit.

I want to encourage you to go against the current and embrace the Lordship of Jesus and His love even in the prophetic. I say this because one of the most beautiful ways you will learn how to hear from God is hearing things in your head that you won't want to do like give money to something or someone you aren't invested in aka the poor or a single mom, you will hear to spend time with people that you don't have the current capacity for, you will make sacrificial decisions that don't make sense unless you look at the model of Jesus in the Bible. As you begin to administrate the prophetic into your life it will shift the way you view your family, lead in an organization church or business, take on the role of husband or wife. You will have a much different process when you hear God because you will be empowered by Jesus who you won't always understand but you will feel compelled by love to obey. The disciples went through this for their first three years of knowing Him but wow the payoff of not just everlasting life but to know Him and see the beautiful plan of God begin to unfold through them as His friends who not only knew His heart from the time they spent with Him but had an outpouring of the same Spirit that is from the Father that Jesus had?! This is what we are going to move into if we will just learn to trust!

My challenge to you as you end this book is to really practice. Practice listening prayer, practice stewarding what you hear from God, practice stewarding prophetic words that are given to you from others, practice the model of revelation/interpretation/application, practicing bringing the prophetic intentionally into your business, church, home, or entertainment career. If we want a different result then the whole world has we have to have a different relationship with God and to His gifts than we currently are having as Christians. It's time to receive from Him in this day and apply what we are hearing in a modern way.

Thank you for reading this! I pray for your journey to be filled with God encounters and that you will take steps to administer and steward what He is telling you.

ACKNOWLEDGMENTS

I want to acknowledge some of the people who made this book possible: (Disclaimer: I know I will miss some in these acknowledgments and I sincerely love those I have missed and value them.)

To my parents, who modeled childlike curiosity for God's Spirit and voice.

To my wife, who encouraged me to train people in the prophetic when I almost walked away from this ministry to be more mainstream.

To Jeremy Butrous, who lovingly helped put together many sections of this book and is my resident theologian and made it possible to see the role of prophets in the Bible the way you get to view them through this book.

Thanks to my Bolz Ministries team, who is Cherie and my biggest support.

Thanks to our church, Expression58, for being our incubator and lab.

To the late great Bob Jones for showing the world that prophecy is married to love

To the late great Jill Austin who I still hear pushing me towards encountering God, not settling for where I am but striving in a healthy way for more.

To the late great David Dreiling, a New York Jewish prophet who took a chance on me and believed that I would be the person I am today.

To the late great John Paul Jackson for taking a risk and publishing my first two books and giving me his audience and esteem.

To the late great Kim Clement who was a fearless prophet and forran part of my calling in Hollywood and on TV and believed in me from the time he met me.

To Paul Cain who prophesied this season and told me all the stories that gave me faith for God to be bigger then I could imagine.

To the prophets who have had such a direct impact on me and my heart and journey: Graham Cooke, James Maloney, Bobby Conner, Cindy Jacobs, Patricia King, Rick Joyner, Kris Volliton, Julie Meyer, Ray Hughes, Larry Randolf, James Goll, Lance Wallnau, Bill Hammond, Lou Engle, John Ekhardt, Jennifer LaClaire, Chuck Pierce, Johnny Enlow,

To the emerging prophets that I get inspired by and have deep relationship with: Julian Adams, Ash Anandi, Gary Morgan, Amy Ward, Jamie Galloway, Justin Allen,

Thanks to the Apostles that I have had the privilege of serving: Bill and Beni Johnson, Che and Sue Ahn, Cal and Michelle Pierce, Randy Clark, Heidi and Roland Baker. (also want to thank Mike and Dianne Bickle who I started with and who taught me so much and who I still love very much.

Thanks to our partners and board members who keep us thriving.

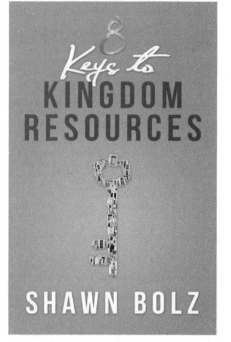

8 KEYS TO KINGDOM RESOURCES

Shawn Bolz presents 8 amazing keys to accessing kingdom resources. God wants you to steward great resources more then you want to.

It is He Who gives you power to get wealth, that He may establish His covenant which He swore to your fathers, as it is this day.
• Deuteronomy 8:18 •

1. Giving and generosity
2. Finance, resources, and time
3. Favor, relationships, and influence
4. Hard word
5. Creativity
6. Education
7. Risk and faith
8. Intimacy with God

KEYS TO HEAVEN'S ECONOMY

So begins the unfolding of Shawn Bolz's visitations from God's heavenly messenger, His minister of finance.

Heavenly resources have only one purpose: that Jesus Christ would receive His full reward and inheritance in our age. Just as God held nothing back from Solomon, who longed to build a tabernacle for God on Earth, God will hold nothing back from a generation of people who long to bring Jesus everything that belongs to Him!

God is about to release finances and resources to reshape the body of Christ on the earth. God is looking for those who desire an open-door experience with the One who is the Master of all keys, Jesus.

Keys to
HEAVEN'S ECONOMY
E-COURSE

DISCOVER THE KEYS TO UNLOCKING YOUR DESTINY

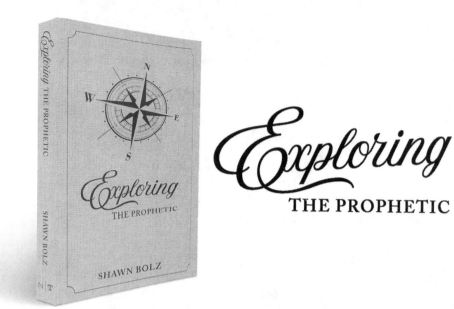

EXPLORING THE PROPHETIC 90 DAY DEVOTIONAL

Learn how to tap into the knowledge of God, hear his voice clearly, and share his words. Cultivate your knowledge of God's heart and mind with these daily intentional steps, deep questions only God can answer, thought-compelling points, and Scripture and questions for personal reflection. Even if the last three months of your life haven't grown your spiritual life much, you can make the next three incredible with the help of this 90-day devotional. Your growth will not only bless those around you; you will also find your own relationship with God transforming into something even more heartfelt and personal than it already is. Read, study, change, and get ready to impact the world.

www.bolzministries.com

PROPHETIC ECOURSE 101
WITH SHAWN BOLZ

AN IN-DEPTH STUDY OF THE PROPHETIC

COURSES.BOLZMINISTRIES.COM

EXPLORING THE PROPHETIC

BE CURIOUS WITH SHAWN BOLZ

WILL FORD
APOSTLE GUILLERMO
JAMES KRAMER
MICHAEL MCINTYRE
BILL JOHNSON
KAREN GIBSON
ANTONY ARIS-OSULA
DOYIN LAYADE
PHIL SMITH
BRIAN HEAD WELCH
TOMMY GREEN
EDWINA FINDLEY
SARA BOWLING
SEAN FEUCHT
AMY WARD
MATT TOMMEY
BOB HASSON
CINDY MCGIL

BOLZ

PODCAST

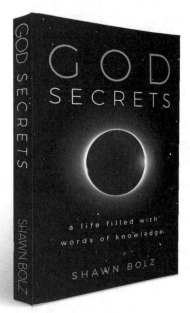

G O D
S E C R E T S

a life filled with
words of knowledge

DID YOU KNOW YOU CAN GROW IN WORDS OF KNOWLEDGE?

Paul encourages believers in 1 Corinthian 14:1, to follow after love and to eagerly desire the gifts of the Spirit, especially prophecy. He would never tell us to pursue something or give us hope for certain gifts if we couldn't engage them! Words of Knowledge is one of the revelatory gifts that we can grow and strengthen just like any other spiritual gift. God loves to tell us specific information about people that we wouldn't naturally know on our own! God has been known to reveal birthdates, anniversaries, family nicknames, pet names, and even bank account numbers at times! The sharing of these personal details help to develop trust and strong connection to the Lord. It produces faith to believe that God deeply loves them and that He truly does have plans to prosper them and give them a hope for their future!

www.bolzministries.com

TRANSLATING GOD

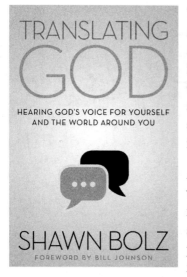

Through a thought-provoking prophetic ministry philosophy and Shawn's glorious successes and very real failures, you will be inspired and equipped to learn how to hear God for yourself and others, grow through simple focused steps, take great risks, stay accountable, love people well, grow in intimacy with the Lord.

As an internationally known prophetic voice who has ministered to thousands, from royalty to those on the streets, Shawn shares everything he has learned about the prophetic in a way that is totally unique and refreshing. Shawn aims for the higher goal of loving people relationally, not just pursuing the gift or information, and he activates you to do the same.

Start to reshape the world around you with God's love today.

TRANSLATING GOD WORKBOOK

Be activated by Shawn's inspirational stories and use the activations, questions, and forms he includes in this life-altering workbook to chart your progress. Either individually or in a group, learn how to:

- Develop your relationship with God and others
- Receive and understand revelation
- Intentionally develop and nurture your prophetic ability
- Become the fullness of God's expression of love through His revelation and voice

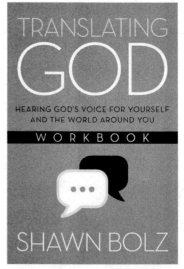

www.BolzMinistries.com

TRANSLATING GOD
STUDY COURSE

GOD IS SPEAKING EVERY DAY,
AND YOU CAN BE HIS MOUTHPIECE.

Sometimes figuring out how to do that can feel overwhelming, but the prophetic can become a completely natural and love-filled part of your life.

You have the chance to help reveal the nature of God and show His heart of love through your prophetic gift. Hearing and sharing His voice are two of the most dynamic and exciting parts of Christianity, and they are actually two of the easiest gifts to pursue.

In this *Translating God* Study Course, Shawn gives you the practical tools you need to further develop your unique strengths and prophetic style. He also shares his insights, personal stories, and profound teaching perspectives to help you:

- Hear God clearly
- Apply God's love-filled revelation to your daily life and relationships
- Increase the depth and effectiveness of your prophetic gift

Translating God will change your perspective of the prophetic and bring depth to your revelation and prophetic voice. Shawn aims for the higher goal of loving people relationally, not just pursuing the gift or information, and he activates you through dynamic exercises that will help you practice doing the same. Great for individuals and group study!

This set includes:
- ° 9 video sessions on 3 DVDs (35-55 minutes each)
- ° *Translating God*: paperback book
- ° *Translating God*: workbook
- ° Poster: to advertise group studies

www.BolzMinistries.com

GROWING UP WITH GOD

Chapter Book

JOIN LUCAS AND MARIA AND FRIENDS
ON THEIR EVERYDAY ADVENTURES IN
FRIENDSHIP WITH GOD!

Lucas knows God talks to him, but he would have never imagined that he would hear such a specific thing about his year . . . and could Maria really have heard God about her destiny? They both have to wonder if God speaks to kids this way. Over the months that follow, God begins to connect them to other kids who grow into friends. Who could have guessed that by the end of the year, their lives would be so exciting!

Award-winning illustrator Lamont Hunt illustrates the rich, vibrant God journey of kids you can relate to. By best-selling author Shawn Bolz.

Workbook

An accompaniment for *Growing Up with God*, the children's chapter book, this workbook will encourage your kids to practice hearing God's voice.

Not only does this workbook teach children how to listen to God, it also gives them the tools they need to support and believe in themselves and each other.

In each section that relates to a chapter in *Growing Up with God*, your children will find:

- A reminder of what was in the chapter
- A true story from a kid their age about how he or she encountered God
- Three important things to know about God's voice
- Bible verses to back up the teaching
- Questions for them to think about and answer
- A prayer
- Illustrations from the book to keep the content focused and exciting

This generation of kids will be the most powerful, prophetic generation yet, and this workbook is a journal and guide that will help them fulfill that destiny.

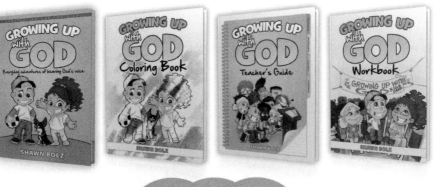